Aglow with The Spirit

aglow
with the
Spirit

Robert C. Frost Ph.D.

VOICE CHRISTIAN PUBLICATIONS, INC.
BOX 672   NORTHRIDGE, CALIFORNIA 91326

Introduction

Several years ago when, with my family, I spent a weekend in Santa Barbara visiting Dr. Frost — then chairman of the Natural Science Division at Westmont College — he began sharing with me the fresh, new personal experience and ministry the Lord was giving him among the students and others in the area.

As he spoke of the scriptural principles behind what was taking place, I was deeply moved. I had thought along this line for some time and had read most of the good books on the subject, but never had I encountered such an approach — I call it an approach in depth — which put the whole matter of *personal* experience with the Holy Spirit into proper relationship with God's deeper purposes in His Son Jesus Christ. Here was a truly *Christ-centered* approach which put this vital piece of the great jigsaw puzzle of *full* salvation into place so it could become — as it really is — a glorious part of the great answer in our lives.

All too often experience in the realm of the Spirit has been made *"a thing in itself."* As such — out of harmony with God's full thought — it can become simply another subtle "It" around which we begin to move. Christ is no longer central and supreme; instead we are caught up into *something else.* This is idolatry in one of its most refined and dangerous forms.

Viewing the fruit in the lives of those affected by Dr. Frost's ministry only confirmed to me the importance of the things the Lord was showing him. Naturally, being an editor, my first thought was, "We must put this into print!" I wanted to see something happen right then and suggested a series of articles for our magazine, *Voice in the Wilderness,* or perhaps some other publication with a larger circulation. But God's time was not ripe, and though Dr. Frost himself was quite willing, somehow the manuscript never got written.

With this background, you can imagine my joy when a few months ago a brief note from Dr. Frost indicated that he had now finished a manuscript, not for an article or two but for a whole book dealing with this subject. With true enthusiasm I entered the details of printing the book. Now, with equal enthusiasm I shall undertake to distribute it, trusting God that it shall find its way into the hearts of thousands who are ready not only to enter but to *develop into maturity* this new and vital dimension of life in Christ.

John Myers, President
VOICE CHRISTIAN PUBLICATIONS

Preface

Every book, like every life, should have a reason for its being. The last few years have witnessed a sovereign and sustained move of the Holy Spirit which has brought the freshness of early New Testament Christianity to searching souls across our nation and even throughout many parts of the world. It has been a growing conviction of ours that the meaning of this move of God should find clear expression in the light of His love for His Son. Every manifestation of the Holy Spirit has significance only as it is related to Jesus Christ.

It is the express desire of the Father that we know the ultimate purpose of His ways in these important days just ahead. Surely God is building His Church for a mighty end-time witness just prior to the return of our Lord. The "living stones" of this Holy Edifice are even now being formed and fitted into their proper place wherever the Holy Spirit is allowed the freedom to move as He would desire. Within such a perspective each life has an important part to play in the fulfillment of God's perfect plan for these closing days of time.

How important it then becomes to be so filled with His Presence that His full will may increasingly find expression through our individual lives. To this end it has been our desire to convey both the significance and the simplicity of entering into the Spirit-filled life by faith. It is our prayer that each reader will come to know the reality of a personal pentecost in his own life before the final pages of this volume have been finished. Indeed, may the power of Holy Spirit Baptism become a motivating and purifying force in all of our lives as we thereby seek to hasten the day of His appearing.

Contents

CHAPTER

PAGE

Introduction

Preface

I. Knowing The Holy Spirit 1

II. God's Will for Me 4

III. God's Way for Me 7

IV. Holy Spirit Baptism 14

V. Why God Chose Tongues 23

VI. God's Parallel Gifts 33

VII. The Role of Faith 43

VIII. Release Your Faith 49

IX. Prayer in The Spirit 65

X. The Spirit and God's Word 74

XI. The Spirit and Our Witness 79

XII. Fellowship in The Spirit 85

XIII. The Spirit of Peace 90

XIV. The Spirit of Holiness 93

XV. The Spirit of Love 103

(Appendix ...... page 107)

CHAPTER I

Knowing the Holy Spirit

A college student once remarked, "To me, the Holy Spirit is nothing more than kind of a white oblong blur !" He was not being irreverent but honest. Many Christians would have to confess, if hard pressed, that to them the Holy Spirit is just about that vague and impersonal. God the Father, they know, God the Son they know, but God the Holy Spirit is unknown to them in any warm personal way. He is considered only as some vague force or influence difficult to apprehend and understand. For many He is the least known and most neglected member of the Holy Trinity.

Others have carefully and systematically studied the nature of the Holy Spirit. They realize that His divine attributes and works place Him in a coordinant rank with the Father and the Son. He is coequal with them and of the same essence; yet in ministry, He is the executive member of the Godhead. Or, as someone has expressed it, *God never moves apart from His Spirit.* It is very possible to delve deeply into the theological aspects of the Holy Spirit and still know Him only as a doctrine. The early New Testament believers never had the privilege or advantage of a course in systematic theology, yet they knew the Holy Spirit in a very powerful and personal way. They were simply "aglow with the Spirit, serving the Lord" (Romans 12:11, Amplified New Testament). God ex-

pects no less of us today if His will for our generation
is to be accomplished.

Do you know Him as they knew Him ? If not, you can
and without delay for God has made every provision for
us to have an experience in the fullness of the Holy Spirit
which is just as fresh and real as was theirs. Thousands
of hungry-hearted Christians of all denominations have
responded to the Spirit's call in recent years and have
found a fellowship with Him which has opened up new
dimensions in both praise and power far beyond their
greatest expectations. God is no respector of persons, and
their experience of fellowship with the Holy Spirit can be
yours today.

How impossible such fellowship would be if the Holy
Spirit Himself were not a person — a warm wonderful
person. As we might expect, there are a number of en-
lightened passages of Scripture which refer to His many
characteristics of personality. We discover that the Holy
Spirit has a mind and a will and can feel (Romans 8:27;
1 Corinthians 12:11; Ephesians 4:30). He can speak,
teach, guide, and comfort (Revelation 2:7; John 14:26;
John 16:13; John 14:16). These and many other refer-
ences plainly indicate that *the Holy Spirit is a real person
and this is why we can know Him in a personal way.*

This privilege of "fellowship and communion" in the
Holy Spirit is profound with meaning (2 Corinthians
13:14; Philippians 2:1). There are some exciting and
fascinating aspects to this which we will discuss in sub-
sequent chapters. At this point, it is interesting to note
that the words "fellowship" and "communion" come from
the same Greek word in the New Testament. The word
is "koinonia" and means *a joint participation around a
common interest.* Communion literally means *a union
around something shared in common.* This obviously raises

a question. If we are going to enjoy communion with and fellowship in the Holy Spirit, what will be the common interest to be shared ? The answer to this question touches on the very purpose for our existence. We will explore this thought further in the next chapter.

CHAPTER II

God's Will for Me

For many years we have taught in the Life Sciences at the collegiate level. In our introductory lectures to freshmen we raise questions concerning the what, when, where, and how of life. We always conclude with the "why" of life. Why are we alive ? What is the purpose of our existence ? Is there an answer to "why are we here ?" Is there any personal meaning to life ? If we can't answer these questions, we have no answers for the most important questions in all of life.

Recently we received a letter from a university student confessing the feeling of futility that he was experiencing living life day by day unrelated to eternal purpose. To him, life was a relentless round of meaninglessness. As I read it, I could not help but wonder how many professing Christians are likewise caught up in a day-by-day sort of existence without any real sense of divine destiny which would link their lives with eternity.

Some years ago we would have had no answer to life's most important questions because we were seeking the answer ourselves. Today, by God's grace, we have the answer. We discovered it in God's Word. We read that God has a plan, a purpose, a divine destiny for every Christian. It was so obviously right when we saw it. *There is only one answer !* In fact, there could be only one answer, for that answer centers in the only begotten Son of the Father. From all eternity past, God the Father has loved God the Son with the love that God is. In the Greek of the New Testament this is "agape" love, "a divine love which is called forth because of the inherent preciousness and worthwhileness of the object loved". *(Wuest.) Anything that answers to the heart of the Father will in some way be related to the Son of His love.*

Man was originally created in His image with the potential of realizing the full will of the Father as it is found in Christ Jesus. Sin entered the heart of man, however, and that image became marred and distorted. Only God knows the pain and disappointment which He experienced at the time of man's fall. God in His grace, however, provided a way whereby once again we could be conformed into the image of His Son. We are told in Romans 8:28,29 that this is our divine destiny, to become like Jesus ! "We are assured and know that all things work together and are fitted into a *plan* for *good* to those who love God and are called according to His *design* and *purpose*. For those whom He foreknew . . . He also *destined* from the beginning to be molded into the image of His Son, that He might become the first-born among many brethren" (Amplified New Testament). *Jesus Christ is the ultimate good toward which all things converge in the life of the Christian.* We are to continually behold and to reflect like mirrors the glory of the Lord and to be constantly transformed into His very own image in ever increasing splendor and from one degree of glory to another (2 Corinthians 3:18, Amplified New Testament). This is the purpose of our existence ! This is the will of our Father.

When the full significance of God's plan for our lives really breaks upon us, it is both amazing and fantastic. To be conformed into the image of God's Son means that we are to *become* as Jesus was; we are to *do* as Jesus did; we are to *think* as Jesus thought; and we are to *speak* as Jesus spoke when He was here on this earth ! In fact, the Lord promised that we would be doing even greater works than these (John 14:12).

As by His Spirit we continue to behold the glory of our Lord, His divine image comes into even sharper focus. The *being* of Jesus speaks of His perfect character and beauty. Jesus is altogether lovely (Song of Solomon 5:16). The *doing* of Jesus relates to His works, power and authority. Jesus was mighty in deed and acted with authority (Matthew 13:54; 21:23,24; Luke 4:36). The *thoughts* of Jesus pertain to the wisdom of God. Jesus is wisdom personified (Proverbs 8:12,14,22,23). The *words* of Jesus speak of the mind and will of God. Jesus is the Word personified (John 1:14).

The word "Christian" means *little Christ !* We are to reflect His beauty, do His deeds, think His thoughts and speak His words. This is what it means to become conformed into the image of Jesus Christ. Do we really understand to what we are committing ourselves when we sing the song, "To be like Jesus . . . All I ask to be like Him"? Actually, we are asking for everything that Jesus is: His character, His work, His mind, His word; His beauty, power, wisdom and will. This is a big order, but it is *our* destiny !

This is what life is all about. To miss this is to miss everything. To gain this is to possess the answer to life's biggest question. Christ is the answer ! God planned it so. *The will of God the Father for you centers in His Son.*

CHAPTER III

God's Way for Me

The revealed will of God for our lives is so wonderful and so perfect that we are amazed and at the same time, if we are honest, somewhat discouraged. Perhaps we have had a secret suspicion all along that the real Christian life was beyond all but a few "superspiritual" individuals who just seemed to be made out of a different kind of stuff than we were anyway. After all, we have given it a try a few times after being sufficiently stimulated by some high-powered speaker, but after a few days or weeks it always wears off and we are left sometimes in worse shape spiritually than we were before. There just doesn't seem to be a "staying power" in our lives that puts us and keeps us dead center in God's will day after day. How quickly the initial thrust fizzles out once we get below the clouds of enthusiasm and hit the earth of daily existence.

How many times we have heard this story in one form or another from people with a deep desire for God's full will but who were almost convinced that it could never be for them. Now such a confession is partly right and partly wrong. Nowhere in the Bible do we find any basis which would support the idea that a victorious Christian life is only for a few chosen people. In one sense there are no super-spiritual Christians, only Christians who have learned how to lean upon the super-natural power of God. Sometimes, in fact, the more "common" the Christian, the easier it is for him to learn how to lean hard upon his God for he is keenly aware of his weaknesses. The Bible is full of common people who lived most "uncommon" lives when they learned the secret of God's way to realizing His will in and through them.

Actually, this is where the problem lies: *we are always substituting our ways for God's ways.* To the extent that we do, we become frustrated and fail. For His ways are not our ways nor ours His (Isaiah 55:8). The Lord then patiently waits for us to come to the end of our road so He can show us His. The individual who in desperation finally confesses that he is just about to give up trying to live the Christian life is closer to God's way than he has ever been before. *If he will look he will find his deadend street is really a crossroads.* The road of "my way" is soon to end. But, the road of "His way" is just to begin.

What is His way? Just as the "will" of the Father centers in a person, the person of God the Son, so the "way" of the Father also centers in a person. It is the person of God the Holy Spirit. *The Holy Spirit is God's way to realizing His will in and through your life.* In Romans 8:28,29 we discovered that it is God's will and our destiny to be conformed into the image of His Son. We found this truth confirmed in 2 Corinthians 3:18. In the last words of this passage we also discover God's way. "Changed into the same image . . . even as by the Spirit of the Lord." In verse 17 of the same chapter we read, "And where the Spirit of the Lord is, there is liberty." Or, as the Amplified New Testament reads: "there is . . . freedom." This means that through the person of the Holy Spirit there is to be a freeing, a liberation, an unleashing, a releasing! Of what? Jesus! All that He *is;* all that He *does;* all that He *thinks;* all that He *says* . . . in us and through us. Hereby we are conformed into His image!

The person and work of the Holy Spirit now begins to take on new and exciting meaning. Here is the Father's *chosen* way and the *only* way He has to make His Son real to and through our lives. Jesus recognized the important role the Holy Spirit was to play in the lives of His disciples (and us) when He talked with them just before His death (John 14, 15, 16). He explained that it was necessary that He go away or the Comforter (the Holy Spirit) would not come. Jesus also knew that the way of departure would cost Him His life. The gift of the Spirit, while freely received on our part, cost God everything He had in His Son. It is not a cheap gift.

The Lord then carefully explained to them the purpose for which the Spirit would be sent. He was about to leave them. Soon, as to His person, Jesus was to be situated at the right hand of the Father in Heaven. What a strange contradiction from the lips of the One who was to say, "Lo, I am with you alway." Strange until we understand the ministry of the Holy Spirit. For Jesus then tells them that when the Comforter would come He would testify (furnish evidence) of Himself (Jesus). That is, He would receive and draw upon that which pertains to Jesus and transmit and reveal this to them in ways that would make His presence and power more real to them than they had ever experienced before. His relationship with them was limited by His physical presence. Then, however, by the Holy Spirit He would be within them fully living His life through them ! Fantastic, but true. True in a life-transforming way.

For illustration look at the picture of Peter before and after the coming of the Holy Spirit on the Day of Pentecost. A boastful, vascillating coward suddenly becomes a humble but powerful preacher on that memorable Feast Day. In fact, with the eye of the Spirit one no longer

hears or sees Peter at all, only Jesus. That is the trans-
forming and conforming power of the Holy Spirit !

No wonder Jesus cautioned His disciples not to go forth
in His name and preach the gospel until after they per-
sonally had received the Holy Spirit in His *fullness.* How
could they preach the *full* gospel until He had first *filled*
their lives ? That is what happened at that first Pentecost
2,000 years ago, and it's happening today in the same way.

Jesus said, "Ye shall receive power after that the Holy
Ghost has come upon you and ye shall be *witnesses* unto
me" (Acts 1:8). One cannot be a witness *for* something
until after he has been a witness *to* something. To witness
something means *to see, to hear, or to directly experience
it;* then one can testify or personally furnish evidence of
that which he has seen and heard. The Greek word for
witness is *martus.* Our word "martyr" is derived from the
same root. To be a true witness is to have experienced
something so real we would be willing to die for it.

In other words Jesus was saying, "The Holy Spirit will
make all that I am so real to you that you will be enabled
to go forth and testify of Me even if it should cost your
life." That is an extremely powerful experience ! No
wonder the early believers turned the then known world
upside down for Jesus Christ. What about our world ?
What about our experience ?

The content of our witness is to show forth the beauty
and power of our Lord's work and Word as we progres-
sively become more like Him. Our lives are to manifest
His *character,* His *work* and His *message.* In ourselves we
are utterly incapable of living such a life and quickly turn
to the provision God has made through the person of the
Holy Spirit. We are going to find that it is by His fruit
and gifts that we are transformed into the image of God's
Son. Let us explore this further.

Just a glance at the fruit of the Spirit as partially listed in Galatians 5:22 and 23 indicates that these are personality characteristics of the Lord Jesus: *Love, joy, peace, longsuffering, gentleness, goodness, faith, meekness and temperance are all vivid word pictures of Christ's character.*

This passage and others which so describe the character of our Lord are showing us how He brings real substance to our Christian faith. The fruit is more than just lovely thoughts. *It is* what Jesus *is !* He *is* love, joy, peace . . . The converse is also true and enhances our appreciation of this truth even further. Love is more than a feeling, Love *is* a person. Likewise, Joy *is* a person; Peace *is* a person. That person *is* Jesus ! Abstract Christianity becomes objective in Christ. The love of God is just as real as *is* God's Son.

The Third Person of the Trinity is also thought of as the Spirit of love, joy, and peace. This is a reflection of His ministry in imparting to us the character of Christ. It is His great desire that we become like Jesus. *If we honor God's Spirit in our lives, He will honor God's Son !*

Let us now look at the nine gifts of the Spirit as outlined in 1 Corinthians 12:7-10. "But the manifestation of the Spirit is given to every man to profit withal. For to one is given by the Spirit the word of wisdom; to another the word of knowledge by the same Spirit; to another faith by the same Spirit; to another the gifts of healing by the same Spirit; to another the working of miracles; to another prophecy; to another discerning of spirits; to another divers kinds of tongues; to another the interpretation of tongues." Again we see God's divine provision which here enables us to think His all-wise and discerning *thoughts,* pray and say His wonderful *words,* and manifest His mighty *works.* How wonderful of God to so equip us that His will in Christ might be realized through us.

Realizing the significance and purpose of the spiritual fruit and gifts, we should be careful never to depreciate them in any way. Their ultimate purpose in expression is to bring us into Christlikeness concerning His character, mind, word, and work. Both the fruit and the gifts are necessary for God's full will. It is possible to manifest either without the other, but impossible for either to have full expression without the other. Both are expressions of God's love and must always be considered as such. First Corinthians 13 clearly indicates that an individual who exercises any of the gifts without love is nothing more than a cipher in the eyes of the Father. However, when they are exercised as expressions of God's love, then His full will finds release in and through our lives. How simple it is to understand God's will and God's way when we see them related to His Son and His Spirit. We shall have more to say about the spiritual fruit and gifts when we share together in the last chapter.

All that has been said thus far presupposes that one has already received the Holy Spirit in His fullness and is enjoying personal fellowship with Him around the Lord Jesus. Just as in the early days of the Church, this is a *definite* experience that has *definite* consequences. Paul's question to the Ephesians, "Have you received the Holy Spirit since you believed?" requires a *definite* answer (Acts 19:2). Something was missing in their lives and Paul quickly detected it. That "something" was the beauty and power of Jesus Christ that always shines forth from a truly Spirit-filled life. Paul's diagnosis of their need was as *definite* as his question was specific and personal.

In a subsequent chapter we will discuss how you can receive the Holy Spirit in His fullness just as they did in the early days of the Church. Thousands of hungry hearts from all backgrounds and denominations are currently finding that God means what He says when He promises us that if we ask we shall receive !

CHAPTER IV

Holy Spirit Baptism

JESUS CHRIST AS OUR SAVIOUR AND BAPTIZER

It is ever the desire of the Holy Spirit to relate our lives to Jesus Christ. Before our conversion to Christ, it was the Spirit who convicted us of our sins and convinced us of our need of a Saviour. These are the elements of true repentance. It was the Holy Spirit who then crowded us to the Cross where we beheld the saving grace of God in Jesus Christ. When we accepted Him as our personal Saviour, it was the Holy Spirit that placed us into the Body of Christ and indwelt us with the life that Christ is. In this sense we are all *indwelt* with the Holy Spirit. We abide in Him, He abides in us. We are new creatures in Jesus Christ. This is the regenerating work of the Holy Spirit. The waters of baptism signify the new life in Christ which is now ours. We now know Jesus Christ personally as our *Saviour.*

We must also know Him, however, as our personal *Baptizer* if the "power" of God's Spirit is to find full expression in our lives. John the Baptist proclaimed that he indeed baptized with water but that One mightier than he was to come, and He would baptize us with the Holy Ghost and with fire (Luke 3:16). Jesus referred to this experience as the "promise of the Father" without which our power for a full witness would be incomplete (Acts 1:4,5,8). *This Baptism is for Power !*

On the Day of Pentecost, 120 expectant people were seated in the Upper Room when suddenly from Heaven

14

the Holy Spirit moved in and upon *each* of them. They were *all* filled with the Holy Ghost and began to speak in other tongues as the Spirit gave them utterance (Acts 2:1-4). The Apostle Peter explained to the amazed on-lookers that that which they "saw and heard" was the promised gift of the Father which Jesus received after His exaltation and which He willingly gives to those who *obediently ask, and receive in faith.* He then prophetically proclaimed that the promise was for *all* who were afar off, even as many as the Lord our God shall call (Acts 2:39). This includes you. This includes me. It is a present tense promise !

BIBLICAL ACCOUNTS OF PERSONAL EXPERIENCES WITH THE HOLY SPIRIT

Let us examine the additional accounts throughout the Book of Acts where the experience of the baptism with the Holy Spirit is witnessed. In the mouth of two or three witnesses shall a matter be established (Deuteronomy 19:15).

A year or so after the coming of the Holy Spirit to the believers in the Upper Room at Jerusalem, Philip went down to the city of Samaria and preached Christ to them (Acts 8:1-25). Many believed and as an outward evidence of the Spirit's regenerating work they were baptized in water. Peter and John then came down from Jerusalem and laid hands upon them for as yet they had not received the Holy Spirit in His fullness. These (except Simon) pre-sumably were people who believed in Jesus with "all their heart" as did the Ethiopian whose experience is recorded in the same chapter. "And Philip said, If thou believest with all thine heart thou mayest (be baptized in water). And he answered and said, I believe that Jesus Christ is the Son of God" (Acts 8:36,37).

It is interesting to note that the word "receive" is derived from the Greek word "lambano". It is not passive in nature and literally means *to take unto oneself*. Here is a beautiful example of the principle that faith actively expresses itself.

One after another they received the Holy Spirit as each one submitted to the laying on of the Apostle's hands. "Then they laid their hands upon them and one by one they received the Holy Spirit" (Acts 8:17, William's Translation). How encouraging to note that *all* the recipients were new converts and that they *all* received one by one.

The account of Simon the magician is interesting in that it indicates that the infilling of the Holy Spirit was accompanied by some tangible evidence which arrested his attention and aroused his ambitions for the "amazing" (Acts 8:12-25, Wuest's Translation). In all probability he saw and heard the same evidence that amazed the onlookers in Jerusalem on the Day of Pentecost.

In Acts 9 we read the account of Saul's conversion. Struck blind by a vision of the Lord, Saul prays and waits in Damascus for Ananias to come and lay his hands upon him that he might be filled with the Holy Spirit and receive his sight. Ananias is a little known man, never heard of in Scripture before or after this occasion. Just a "common" man but with a very "uncommon" mission to fulfill. How encouraging this can be to most of us. Obedient to the Spirit's leading, he visits Saul, addresses him as his brother in Christ and lays his hands upon him that Saul too may enter into the fullness of the Holy Spirit. One is impressed with the Holy Spirit's desire to immediately fill new converts with His presence.

Some six years later the Holy Spirit instructs Peter (somewhat against his wishes) to carry the full gospel of God's grace to a people he had always considered to be unclean (Acts 10). God in His amazing love always has a way of looking at men's hearts rather than at the barrier of outward appearances which sometimes so easily separates us. The Gentile household of Cornelius in Caesarea had both receptive hearts and open minds to Peter's message. This was all that was necessary for God to honor His Word in their lives. And honor His Word He did, for just as Peter was speaking, the gift of the Holy Spirit in His fullness was outpoured upon "all them that heard the word" (Acts 10:44, 45).

It was the same experience that Peter had on the Day of Pentecost for they too "spake with tongues and magnified God" (Acts 10:46). Peter was satisfied that their experience was genuine, and immediately baptized them in water. The Jews at Jerusalem, however, were skeptical until Peter shared with them what he had "seen and heard" (Acts 11:1-8). Then, the Scripture declares, "they held their peace and glorified God." What a beautiful example for all of God's people to follow as once again in our time we see God's Spirit being outpoured upon *all* flesh !

The last account in our series occurs 20 years after the initial coming of the Holy Spirit in His fullness to the 120 in the Upper Room at Jerusalem. It is found in Acts 19:1-7.

The Apostle Paul stops at Ephesus on his way to Jerusalem to complete his third and last missionary journey. There he finds a group of 12 disciples in whose lives a dimension was missing. With keen spiritual discernment Paul quickly diagnoses the need and abruptly asks them a simple but pointed question: "Have ye received the Holy Ghost since ye believed ?"

What prompted such a question ? What was so obviously lacking ? There is both a beauty and a power to life that comes in joyfully praising God. *The Holy Spirit is the Spirit of praise and power!* I wonder if the meeting may have been a little on the gray, weak, and gloomy side. Perhaps Paul sensed that the "oil of gladness" and the "power of the Spirit" were missing.

They quickly confessed that the person of the Holy Spirit was indeed a stranger to them. They had entered into John's baptism of repentance and had turned away from the world but had not entered into the abundant life of praise and power which Jesus had promised. One wonders how many Christians today have proceeded no further than this halfway mark.

Paul preaches Jesus to them, and they are then baptized in Jesus' name as an outward testimony of their new life in Christ. Paul then proceeds to introduce them to the person of the Holy Spirit in His fullness. After the laying on of his hands, the Holy Spirit comes upon them and they "spake with tongues and prophesied." Once again we see the now twenty-year-old pattern repeated. *"Repent, be baptized, and thou shalt receive!"*

One is impressed with the rather natural way the Scriptures unify our concept of salvation by repeatedly linking together the elements of *repentance* (conversion), *baptism* (water), and *reception* (Holy Spirit in full power). This seems to be the New Testament pattern: repentance — baptism — reception. The foundation for redemption in its full sense, both theologically and experimentally, is incomplete without all three. Each element is but a segment of one great work of grace.

Regeneration is related to repentance in the conversion experience. At this time, as mentioned before, the Holy Spirit indwells us as the Spirit of Christ. We are infused with the "life" of Christ. We are also baptized by the Holy Spirit into the Body of Christ (1 Corinthians 12:13).

Hereby we enter into a close inter-personal relationship with our Lord. He abides in us and we abide in Him. The Holy Spirit has identified us with the life and person of God's Son. It is interesting to note that in the conversion experience it is *the Spirit that baptizes us into Christ.*

In water baptism a member of the body of Christ baptizes the new believer in water. This is a consumating witness to one's faith in Christ and is symbolic of the washing of regeneration which occurs at conversion. It is also a picture of the death and burial of the "old man" with Christ Jesus and the coming forth as a new creature with Him unto resurrection life.

Water baptism also is a prophetic picture of the baptism with the Holy Spirit which should immediately follow. We find according to John the Baptist that *Christ is to baptize the new believer into the Holy Spirit.* "I indeed baptize you with water unto repentance . . . but he (Christ) shall baptize you with the Holy Ghost" (Matthew 3:11). The new convert is not only to be indwelt with the Holy Spirit, but he is to be filled within and flooded without. There is a "within" and an "upon" relationship with the Holy Spirit which will endue the new believer with "power" to witness. "And ye shall receive power after that the Holy Ghost has come *upon* you and ye shall be witnesses unto me." "And they were all *filled* with the Holy Ghost and they spake the word of God with boldness" (Acts 4:31).

This experience should normally follow water baptism rather closely. We know of a church in California which has had a remarkable ministry to the Japanese fieldworkers who are over here on short term visas. God has beautifully overcome the language barrier and scores have come to find the Lord Jesus as their Saviour. They also discover rather quickly that He is their Baptizer as well, for most of them are filled with the Holy Spirit as they arise from the baptismal waters. It is a beautiful sight to see them come forth praising and magnifying God in other languages as the Spirit giveth utterance. Surely this is very close to the New Testament pattern.

Just as the pattern would not be complete if repentance were not followed by baptism, so is the pattern incomplete if baptism is not followed by the receiving of God's Spirit in His fullness for power. This was the normal and expected procedure in early New Testament Christianity. Although each redemptive element might be (and usually is) separated briefly in time, as far as personal participation and appropriation is concerned, they are still but different aspects of one great work of salvation. Perhaps this is the reason the epistles sometimes make little distinction between baptism into Christ's body, water baptism, and the baptism with the Holy Spirit. Theologically these are all integral parts of the same redemptive foundation upon which the Christian life is to be built.

The indwelling Spirit brings life, but the fullness of the Spirit brings power. This latter element of the basic New Testament pattern is sadly missing in most of modern Christianity. The full force of God's great redemptive work is frustrated. The life of the Church is *weakly* expressed. In practice a period has been placed after "repent and be baptized." No longer is baptism followed by the laying on of hands for the fullness of God's Spirit in power. The rite of confirmation most closely follows the form, but even here no one really expects to receive and to respond as did the disciples at Ephesus under Paul's ministry (Acts 19:1-7).

The present day outpouring of the Holy Spirit in fullness for power is once again completing the foundation upon which the Church is to be built. There is only one foundation for the Church. That foundation is *Christ*. Once again His dual role as *Saviour* and *Baptizer* is being recognized as personally essential for God's full redemptive purpose.

As we again review the various accounts in the Book of Acts where the experience of the baptism with the Holy Spirit is witnessed, several interesting things come to our attention. First of all, in every case *all* who were open and seeking were filled. All 120 in Jerusalem, all in Samaria, all at Cornelius' house and all twelve at Ephesus. No one was left out. It was for all — and it still is ! "For the promise is unto you . . . and to all that are afar off" (Acts 2:39).

Secondly, after the Day of Pentecost we find that every individual in all of the remaining accounts were *new* converts. They had either just been baptized in water or were baptized right after receiving the fullness of the Holy Spirit. It is as if God is trying to impress us with the fact that from the very beginning of our Christian life He cannot completely *fulfill* His will in our lives without first *filling* us with His Spirit. So simple, so obvious, so right, yet how many Christians can definitely answer Paul's question to the Ephesians in the affirmative ?

Thirdly, we discover that the Holy Spirit in His fullness was always received in faith after or as the Word of the Lord was ministered. *The Holy Spirit always confirms our faith in God's Word !*

Lastly, we find in each case, directly recorded or indirectly implied, that related with the infilling experience was an *outward evidence* of praise in an unlearned heaven-sent language. Why would God repeatedly choose to uniquely link this particular manifestation of the Spirit with the initial infilling experience ? We have the right to inquire as did the onlookers at the Day of Pentecost concerning what they *saw and heard*. "What meaneth this ?" There is great significance in the answer to this question as we shall shortly see. In fact, we do not willfully ignore any purposeful pattern that God chooses to reveal ! There is meaning and significance in God's choices and ultimately we know they will be related to the Lord Jesus Christ, the Son of His love.

CHAPTER V

Why God Chose Tongues

Man is the highest form of God's creative majesty. Only man was created in His image. Only man has the capacity for conceptual thought. Only man has the power to project his mind in meaningful communication with others. The ability to think and communicate with others is related to man's capacity to manipulate word symbols. The Genesis record indicates that at his creation man was endowed with the gift of conceptual thought and speech. Here is the *symbol of the soul.* "For as he thinketh in his heart, so is he" (Proverbs 23:7). "Out of the abundance of the heart the mouth speaketh" (Matthew 12:34). Here is the divinely given instrument by which man as a free moral agent may bless or blaspheme, may praise or curse. No wonder James implies that *the power which can tame the tongue can tame the man!* (James 3). When God related the manifestation of tongues with the fullness of the Spirit in the Book of Acts, He chose an evidence that reaches down and touches the very "citadel" of man's being. What a beautiful and powerful picture: *the complete surrender of the soul to the Spirit's control.* "And they were all filled with the Holy Ghost and began to speak with other tongues as the Spirit gave them utterance" (Acts 2:4).

As always, when the Spirit is in control, one's attention is directed to God in praise and worship. "We do hear them speak in our tongues the wondrous works of God"

(Acts 2:11). "For they heard them speak in tongues and magnify God" (Acts 10:46). Furthermore, this privilege of "divinely inspired praise" is to find continual daily expression in our devotional life.

While not all may be called upon by faith to exercise the gift of tongues for the edification of the Body of Christ in group worship (1 Corinthians 12:30), Paul clearly indicates the use of "devotional tongues" is for all. Just as the initial outward evidence was for *all* at Jerusalem, Samaria, Caesarea and Ephesus, so Paul desires that his hearers might *all* sing and pray in the Spirit in their private worship (1 Corinthians 14:5,15). *It is a God-given means by which our faith in the faithfulness of God's infilling Spirit can always find expression !* It is a divinely-given way for preventing an experience from becoming a one-time affair which fades out into the past as time moves on. Rather, here is a daily contact with God which keeps the significance of His Son fresh in our minds and real in our hearts.

THE MEANING OF DEVOTIONAL TONGUES TO MAN

Let us develop this thought further. The Apostle Paul indicates that there is a two-fold meaning to devotional tongues. Firstly, on the "manward" side Paul declares that we are by-passing the *limitations of our minds,* for in the Spirit we are speaking "mysteries" (1 Corinthians 14:2). How often our greatest assets can become our greatest liabilities when it comes to certain dimensions in the Spirit. One of God's greatest gifts to mankind is the human mind. Yet, what a barrier it can sometimes be when the ways of God are involved. I have discovered that one of our greatest problems in the Christian life is related to our trying to *outplan, outguess, outthink* and even *outpray*

God. Isaiah rather sharply defines the problem in the
words of the Lord Himself, "For my thoughts are not
your thoughts, neither your ways my ways . . . For as the
heavens are higher than earth, so are my ways . . . and my
thoughts than your thoughts" (Isaiah 55:8,9).

How good of God to provide a way of His choosing
whereby we can bypass our limited understanding when
we know not how to pray. With great sensitivity Paul
shares this truth with us in the following words: ". . . the
Spirit, too, is helping us in our weakness for we do not
know how to pray as we should, but the Spirit Himself
pleads for us with unspeakable yearnings, and He who
searches our hearts knows what the Spirit thinks, for He
pleads for His people in accordance with God's will"
(Romans 8:26,27, Williams' Translation). Paul further
reinforces this thought on another occasion when he clear-
ly indicates that it is both our privilege and responsibility
to pray "with the Spirit" as well as "with the understand-
ing" (1 Corinthians 14:15).

There have been times perhaps when all of us have
been moved by heavy burdens of confession or interces-
sion and the deep yearnings of our hearts far transcended
our powers to express them in any articulate way. And,
even if we could have, we would not have known how
to pray "in accordance with God's will." How gracious
of God to provide every Spirit-filled believer a "heavenly
way" when prayer in an earthly language fails to convey
the deep cry in our hearts. Truly at such times real satis-
faction can only come as "deep calleth unto deep" and
the Spirit Himself pleads for us.

I remember a close friend of ours confiding to me that
after the sudden death of his wife, there converged upon
him and his little family a variety of discouraging and
depressing problems. There were such times of despair

that he could only gain release as he yielded himself to the Holy Spirit in prayer. Through a heaven-sent language of love God would again and again bring peace to his heart. How great is God's grace !

There is also the testimony of a housewife through whom God interceded in a most unusual way. She was washing dishes when a heavy burden of intercession came upon her. She dried her hands and immediately began to pray in a heavenly language for someone, somewhere, whom she did not know. Finally the release came and she felt that God had answered her Spirit-inspired prayer. A short time later, a returned missionary shared with her that at that particular hour they had been in great distress and were crying out to the Lord for deliverance. How wonderful and wise are God's ways in meeting the needs of His people !

There is another aspect to devotional tongues which we also find very meaningful to man. The Scripture indicates that praying in tongues is a God-given means by which the individual can edify or build himself up (1 Corinthians 14:4). It is interesting to note that the phraseology which the Apostle Paul uses in this passage indicates that here is something, by God's Spirit, that we can *choose* to do that will build us up in Jesus Christ. Here is one way the Holy Spirit progressively fashions our lives into the image of God's Son. Furthermore, there is a divine awareness of His conforming touch upon our lives when we pray in the Spirit. This is something that cannot be objectively analyzed, only subjectively experienced.

The freshness of His presence during such times of devotional prayer keeps our Christian experience from ever growing stale. Here is a real source of "staying power !" It is with good reason that one senses a spirit of determination in the words of Paul when he declares, "I *will*

pray . . . and sing with the spirit . . . and with the under-
standing also" (1 Corinthians 14:15,16).

There is still another dimension on the manward side
which is worthy of our consideration. The Bible declares
that "where the Spirit of the Lord is, there is liberty" (2
Corinthians 3:17). Liberation of what ? Well, obviously
from our previous remarks the only thing the Holy Spirit
is interested in releasing is the beauty and power of Jesus
Christ in us. Now this liberty begins with our worship.
*There is a releasing power in praise that influences our
entire being and carries over into every area of life ex-
perience.* The Holy Spirit is the spirit of worship and the
content of the heavenly language is primarily praise dur-
ing times of devotion.

If your life seems tight and tense there is both rest and
release in praise. Praying in tongues is a means of releas-
ing our spirits, and where the spirit is free, the heart and
mind can follow.

I remember a young lady visiting a prayer-and-share
group in our home a couple of years ago. When prayer
time came, she immediately entered into the fullness of
the Holy Spirit by faith and spontaneously burst forth in
a beautiful heavenly language of praise. There then fol-
lowed a rather marked change in her whole personality.
Where before she had been bound in spirit and discour-
aged in heart, she at once experienced a whole new life
of freedom. It was obvious to her classmates, teachers, and
family. She discontinued her counseling sessions with the
school psychologist for there was no further need. The
last time we visited with her over two years later, she
was still joyful in the Lord and growing in God's good-
ness. *Truly, where the Spirit of the Lord is, there is liberty !*

It is the ministry of the Holy Spirit to bring such re-
lease to our lives when by faith we allow Him to fill us

to overflowing with praise to the One who has set us free. "If the Son therefore shall make you free, ye shall be free indeed" (John 8:36). May we say it again, *"There is a definite releasing power in praise."* No wonder the Apostle Paul exclaims with great feeling "I thank my God I speak in tongues more than ye all !"

THE MEANING OF DEVOTIONAL TONGUES TO GOD

Let us now direct our attention to the significance of devotional tongues as related to the "Godward" side. We discover again from Paul's inspired writings that we are giving thanks well when we praise the Lord with His Spirit (1 Corinthians 14:16,17). Such divinely directed praise and worship to God's Son is well pleasing to the Father. *Praise is God-pleasing !*

Sometime ago I searched the Scripture for additional passages which indicate how God feels concerning our worship. At first I was disappointed for I found only a few verses which seemed pertinent. Then one evening one of my students came to our home for spiritual counsel with my wife and me. I was going to share some passages from the Psalms in the *Amplified Old Testament,* when the Lord clearly prompted me to share selected passages from the Song of Solomon. As I did, it suddenly dawned upon us that here was an entire book that dealt with the deep *desire* of God that His great love for us might find its completion and return in our worship. The shepherd boy and his bride-to-be present a beautiful picture of Christ and His bride the Church. Just as the heart of the shepherd boy *yearned* to hear the voice of his beloved, so the Lord Jesus delights in hearing our love for Him expressed by our praise. "Thy lips, O my spouse, drop as the honeycomb: honey and milk are under thy tongue" (Song of Solomon 4:11). The "sacrifice of praise" and the "fruit of our lips" are as sweet incense to our wonderful Lord (Hebrews 13:15; Psalm 141:2).

There is nothing more satisfying or significant in all of life than to recognize and express the worth-ship of Almighty God. Yet, who hasn't in times of deep devotion found he was unable to find words to express the great longings of his soul for God ? How good of God to give us such a beautiful gift. What a marvelous expression of His love to us that our love for Him might find full expression in return.

It was our privilege in my office to lead a young seminary student and his fiancee into the fullness of God's Spirit some time ago. Following a sweet time of worship and praise together in the Spirit, the young man remarked, "I have been very close to this heavenly release in my devotions many times. I would come to a place where words failed and all I could do was to sigh in the Spirit. If I had known then what I know now, I could have easily yielded my lips and tongue to God in this heavenly expression of praise."

The Lord is supremely "pleased" with our expressions of praise and worship — much more so, I sometimes think, than we realize. In fact, Proverbs 15:8 tells us that God is actually "delighted" with our prayers: ". . . the prayer of the upright is his delight." The dimension of praise in devotional tongues is most meaningful to God for "thou verily givest thanks well" (1 Corinthians 14:17). Our praise is well-pleasing to the Father. I am sure the Apostle Paul would be one of the first to join his voice with ours in the words of the magnificent hymn, "O for a Thousand Tongues To Sing My Great Redeemer's Praise !"

A SYMBOL OF SURRENDER

There is yet another symbolic meaning found in this God-given and God-chosen manifestation of the Holy Spirit. It is that of divine control ! As we read the record of the first Pentecost, we find that they spoke "as the Spirit gave them utterance" (Acts 2:4). *That* they spoke was not supernatural: it was their lips, their tongues, and their voices. But *what* they spoke was supernatural, for the Spirit was in divine control. This is a forceful picture of how the Spirit of Holiness desires to take and control not only this our most unruly member but every member of our being to the praise and honor and glory of God's Son. Here we see a wedding of all that God is with all that we are (and are not) to accomplish His divine purpose. *In His great grace He has chosen to work out His perfection through our imperfection, if we will submit ourselves without reservation to the perfecting power of His Spirit.*

A medical student and his fiancee were seated together hand-in-hand in my office one Saturday morning asking questions about the gift of the Holy Spirit for their lives. We had shared with them the seriousness of surrendering our lives to the control of the Holy Spirit. We had explained that God was ready to meet the desires of their hearts for His fullness as soon as they were ready to ask God to so honor His Word. The young man became very serious and then said, "I am afraid if I ask the Holy Spirit to take over my life, that He will want me to give something up that I don't want to give up." At first I thought it might have been his ambitions for the medical profession, but he indicated otherwise. "No," he said, "it's not that. I'm afraid He will make me give up ——— (his fiancee's name)." They sat there hand-in-hand with tear-filled eyes. I realized that the significance of surrendering everything to the Holy Spirit had been taken very seriously. They were not entering into an experience lightly without realizing the full meaning involved.

We then shared with them that God in His love for them had led them together in their love for one another. We explained that the Holy Spirit had united them in Christ and that He was now requesting that their first allegiance would always *first* be to Him and *then* to each other. This way they would always be one in God's will and purpose for their lives. The Holy Spirit of unity never wanted them to be divided when it would come to such an important issue. Jesus was not only to be their Saviour, but their Lord, forever and always. Still hand-in-hand they bowed their heads in surrender to God, and lifted their hearts in expectant faith for the fullness of God's Spirit. The presence of God literally filled the room and two young lives were united in a Spirit of praise and worship in a heavenly way which they had never enjoyed together before. *There is a holy beauty in the surrender of the soul !*

How absolutely faithful God is to those who obediently "empty" their lives for His "fullness." In fact, one sees rather quickly that initially and progressively the "cross" of self-emptying always accompanies the "crown" of the Spirit's infilling. The proud self-centered person would never in faith have submitted himself to the hands of the Apostles for the fullness of the Holy Spirit in early New Testament times. Others did, however, and the then known world was turned upside down. Oh, that our world might be so shaken ! There are repeated indications that it may happen, for as the Apostle Paul humbled himself at the hands of Ananias that he might be filled with the Holy Spirit (Acts 9:17), so many today are humbling themselves before the hand of God and finding, much to their joy, that the heavenly pattern for spiritual power and holiness has not changed.

CHAPTER VI

God's Parallel Gifts

It is always inspiring to read of God's faithfulness in the lives of others, but it is even more wonderful to realize that God desires to do the same for anyone who will simply take Him at His Word. God is no respector of persons ! The heavenly Dove of God's Spirit waits expectantly for us to open our hearts to the fullness of His presence. He desires to wing His way into every area of our lives if we will but give Him the invitation. *He is gentle and will not force His desire upon us but will swiftly alight upon the life of one whose hand of faith beckons for His infilling presence.*

Perhaps you are interested in the fullness of God's Spirit for your life but are not sure what the simple way of faith really is. It is our purpose in the paragraphs to follow to help you in releasing your faith in God's Word. As you do, *you* are going to find that God will honor your faith by confirming His Word in your life. If you are willing, He is fully prepared to do this even before you have completed reading this book ! Let us begin in a simple way by comparing the Gift of God's Son with that of His Spirit. There are many meaningful parallels.

BOTH GIFTS ARE RECEIVED BY FAITH

Both are gifts of God's grace and appropriated by faith alone (Ephesians 2:8,9; Galatians 3:2,14). It is not neces-

sary to beg God for a gift He has already given, but rather
to believe and receive with thanksgiving the "given gift."
The simplicity of something so right, so real and so easily
entered into is disarming. In fact, the Adversary will im-
mediately flood our minds with a host of doubts and reser-
vations; for he knows the moment we step out in faith
without hesitation, God *will* fulfill His promise !

BOTH GIFTS ARE RELATED TO SIMILAR DOUBTS

The doubts and questions all fall into a similar pattern
for both the Gift of God's Son and the Gift of God's
Spirit. All are devilishly designed to undermine our faith.
All can effectively be met by God's Word, which the
Spirit honors as the source and basis of our faith. God's
faithfulness is *not* related to how "we think" or how "we
feel," but *what He has said* ! Jesus said, "If anyone (this
is for all) is thirsty (recognize his need for the Springs
of the Spirit), let him come to me (Jesus is our Saviour
and Baptizer) and drink (obedience in action). Whoever
(again, for all) continues to believe in Me (as Saviour
and Baptizer) will have as the Scripture says (faith in
God's Word), rivers (gifts and graces) of living water
continuously flowing from within him (a daily experi-
ence). By this He referred to the Spirit (God's way to
his will) that those believing in Him were going to re-
ceive (the Promise Given)" (John 7:37-39, Williams'
Translation).

The Problem of Fear

Many miss God's greatest gifts because of fear. Some
are afraid of "other people," fearful of what "they" may
say or do or think. Certainly, as we become more like
Jesus we can expect both ridicule and persecution. Jesus
said so ! But, in another passage the Lord encouraged us

with the promise that we will not stand alone when it comes to our witness for Him. By our side will be "the Comforter (Counselor, Helper, Advocate, Intercessor, Strengthener and Standby)" (John 15:26,27; Amplified New Testament). Anything that draws us closer to Christ will also draw criticism from those who do not understand. We need only look to our own lives in times past when God has desired to bring about a Christlike change that we did not understand. How critical we were at first until the Spirit of Truth finally melted our reservations and we saw a new dimension of His love. His love has a way of ultimately making its mark. *This is to be our only defense, the love of God.* And, it really works ! Furthermore, where perfect love is there is *no* fear.

Others are afraid of the "unknown," even in God. I suppose there is natural awe and wonder to new dimensions in God which we all have sensed. Whenever men in Holy Scripture encountered the presence of God, they fell to the ground in Holy fear. The holiness of Almighty God commands our respect and reverence and rightly so. Yet, at such times, God's response was always one of love. Over and over again, His words of comfort would come, "Fear not." We are not to be afraid of new experiences in God which are scriptural, but accept them as gifts of His love. What fear we have is not from Him for, "God hath not given us the spirit of fear; but of power, and of love, and of a sound mind" (2 Timothy 1:7). *To love is to trust ! Fear is really the product of unbelief.*

It was our privilege some time ago to share our testimony with a godly Mission Covenant minister and his wife. His hunger and interest in the Holy Spirit in His fullness were dampened by a fear. On several occasions when he had preached on Satan and his deceptive ways he had been hindered by personal sickness or other dis-

ruptive occurrences. Knowing personally the power of the
Evil One from experience, he was afraid that if he pas-
sively opened his life to the spiritual realm some evil
might enter his life. The Lord quickly gave us both the
answer from the Word:

First of all, we are not "passively" opening ourselves
to the spirit realm. *Faith is active and definite !* It is char-
acterized by its object. Our faith is in God and *His* Word.
We are coming to *Him* at *His* invitation. We are seeking
His Spirit that we might glorify *His* Son. The Father has
promised the Holy Spirit in His fullness to those who
would ask. God would no more allow an evil spirit to
harm a sincere seeker than an earthly father would give
a serpent to his son when he had requested a fish (Luke
11:9-13). Just as we confidently open the door of our
hearts to Jesus at salvation so do we open our lives to
God's Spirit for His fullness without fear.

The minister then arose from his desk, knelt in prayer,
confessed his faith in God's Word, and immediately lift-
ed his voice in a heavenly language of praise. After we
had worshipped the Lord for a time together, he expressed
how God's infilling and overflowing presence had a
warmth and a softness that brought an inner glow of
peace and rest. How Satan would deceive us by fear if
he could !

On another occasion a young college athlete who was
then one of my students came to our home with the ex-
press interest in knowing more about the Holy Spirit.
We had shared together from God's Word for a couple
of hours. Then he said, "You know, I believe the Lord
has brought me here this evening and that this is for me,
but I feel so 'apprehensive' inside." We assured him the
Holy Spirit was a gentleman and would not force His way
into his life. We suggested that if he wanted to read God's

Word further or pray some more we would understand. We also told him that if he decided to stay, God would immediately honor his faith. He stayed and raised a few additional questions reflecting his continuing concern. Finally, I suggested that we pray and allow the Holy Spirit to "wash out" of his life the fear and apprehension and replace it with His joy and peace. We prayed together and the Lord faithfully filled him with His Spirit. He softly worshiped the Lord for some time in his new language in the Spirit. Finally he looked up and his first words in English were these, "Peace I leave with you, my peace I give unto you: not as the world giveth, give I unto you" (John 14:27). "Dr. Frost," he said, "I have never experienced such peace as this in all my life." Here indeed was the "peace that passeth all understanding."

The Problem of Reason

Some hold back because they cannot rationalize their way into an apprehension of God's gifts. "I just don't understand it all" is a familiar phrase. Fortunately, we don't have to, because God's ways always go beyond the limitations of our understanding anyway. In His grace He has provided a way which is reasonable, but not limited by reason. It is the way of faith. *Faith can realize in experience what the mind cannot comprehend through reason alone !*

If we had to wait until we "understood" all about salvation before accepting Christ as our Saviour, we could never be converted. Fortunately, it's enough to know our need and His supply and actively accept and confess them both by faith in God's Word. God does the rest and confirms our faith in experience. Salvation becomes a real gift and we can know that it is our possession !

The same principle applies to the Gift of God's Spirit.

We have a need for spiritual power, and in His grace God has provided a supply. We may not understand it all; but through God's way of faith, it can become our possession and we will know it experientially.

One evening we shared some of these thoughts concerning the Holy Spirit with one of my college students. He asked a great many questions for there was much which he did not understand and he wanted a reasonable basis on which to rest his faith. Finally, he was ready to take God at His Word and indicated his desire to pray. We laid hands upon him and prayed for God to fill his life to overflowing. As he lifted his voice in expectant faith, the infilling Holy Spirit gave him a new language of praise. After we had worshiped the Lord together for a time in this newfound way, he remarked, "You know, when I came here tonight I was afraid I might get 'psyched up' into something that wasn't real. But it really is real, isn't it?" How wonderful that *God always confirms His Word in experience.*

On another occasion a young college fellow came to our home to discuss the validity of the Pentecostal experience. He too asked a great many questions, but finally confessed that he just couldn't "see" it. It was simply beyond his understanding.

His background teaching had been aggressively antagonistic to the possibility that God would still fill people with the Holy Spirit just as we read in the Book of Acts. I suggested that we pray together and ask God to lead us into His full truth for our lives. We also prayed that if this were real and for him, God would increase his desire and make him restless until he found his full satisfaction in a genuine Pentecostal experience. If it was not real, we prayed the desire and interest would fade away as time progressed. We indicated to him that if God is really pouring out His Spirit as we believe He is, he would be continually bumping into "Spirit-filled" Christians wherever he went. This was at the end of the school year and he didn't return to college in the fall. It was two years before our paths crossed again. We had been invited to the home of some Spirit-filled Plymouth Brethren in Los Angeles. To our pleasant surprise, our young friend was present. God had faithfully allowed his life to repeatedly cross the lives of other Christians who had found this new dimension in the Holy Spirit. Their Christlike love had convinced him of the validity of their Pentecostal experience.

Just before he left, he shared with me his hunger of heart and newfound openness of mind. We briefly outlined the simple way of faith to God's gifts. He indicated that he was ready for God's all and expected the Holy Spirit to control both his life and his lips for God's glory. He then wondered if he could enter into the Spirit of praise in his own private devotions. We assured him of God's faithfulness and encouraged him to take Him at His Word. Once again our paths parted but this time we both sensed a spirit of great expectation. Some day our lives may cross again. When they do, I know it will be an occasion for our rejoicing together in the Lord for His faithfulness. Truly, God has a way of over-ruling the limitations of our minds when we humbly seek Him in His fullness.

The Problem of So-called Hypocrites

Occasionally the lives of those who have entered into these Gifts of God have proven to be stumbling blocks to honest inquirers. Unbelievers point to so-called "hypocrites" and "failures" in the churches. To depreciate a gift or the Giver because of what an individual does or does not do with it hardly seems fair. This is true both for the Gifts of God's Son and His Spirit.

The evidence of what God can do through a life will not be found in those who have "moved in" and then "backed off." In such a life the Holy Spirit is *grieved* and His power and purpose *quenched*. Fortunately, many choose to "move on" and their lives, under the continual control of the Spirit and the Word, become real testimonies of God's grace and power. Such individuals would be quick to direct our attention from themselves to the Lord Jesus, who is the lovely and powerful pattern for their lives. May their ideal become ours as well.

We must also realize as indicated earlier that neither the Gifts of God's Son nor His Spirit are marks of our maturity. Rather, they are expressions of His grace whereby we can progressively fulfill His perfect will for our lives. *God takes us where we are that by His Spirit we may become like He is !*

The Problem of God's Chosen Symbols

Many times the question arises, "Do I *have to* speak in tongues to be filled with the Holy Spirit ?" The answer to the question so phrased would be emphatically no ! *The gift never brings the Giver.* This is getting the cart before the horse. The next question then is usually, "Will everyone who is filled with the Holy Spirit always speak in tongues ?" The answer to this is simply that God is sovereign and can do anything anyway He wants. But, *why* seek a way outside of a meaningful pattern which He Himself has chosen and recorded in His Word ?

Perhaps a better question would be, "May I enter into the *same* experience in the *same* way as I see it recorded in the Scriptures ?" To this every promise of faith in the Book would emphatically cry "Yes !"

BOTH INVOLVE AN INWARD WORK AND
AN OUTWARD EXPRESSION

Having considered some of the more common questions about the Pentecostal experience, let us further pursue the parallel between the Gifts of God's Son and God's Spirit. As we do, we make the fascinating discovery that both involve an "inward work" and an "outward expression." The Scriptures declare that, "with the *heart* man believeth unto righteousness" (Romans 10:10). This is the inward work. Then there is an outward confession or evidence of this inward work for "with the *mouth* confession is made unto salvation." This is the outward confirmation that the conversion experience has found its consummation. It is a beautiful confession of God's faithfulness. *Furthermore, the outward confession confirms, crystalizes, and catalyzes the inward work !* Every day that we confess that Jesus is Lord to ourselves, to others, and to God, the inward work is further strengthened and established.

The same is true in the Gift of God's Spirit in His fullness. First, by faith and with a heart full of worship, we appropriate the infilling presence. Then we lift our voices to the control of the Holy Spirit who will direct our confession heavenward in a divinely-given language of praise. "And they were all *filled* with the Holy Ghost and began to *speak* with other tongues as the Spirit gave them utterance" (Acts 2:4). Tongues is the *outward* evidence of the *inward* work. Furthermore, this too is an active expression of our faith which at a point in time crystalizes and catalyzes the inward work. Every day as one prays in this divinely given way it is a continual *reaffirmation* of one's surrender by faith to the full control of God's indwelling

Spirit. *Here is a beautiful, meaningful privilege for all Christians !* It is ours for the asking, when we ask in faith.

CHAPTER VII

The Role of Faith

Faith Is the Key that Unlocks the Door to God's Gifts. Faith is the key to our entire Christian experience. By *faith* are we saved ! "For by grace are ye saved through faith" (Ephesians 2:8). By *faith* are we filled ! "That we might receive the promise of the Spirit by *faith*" (Galatians 3:14). By *faith* do we pray with the Spirit in devotional tongues. "And these signs shall follow them that *believe* . . . they shall speak with new tongues" (Mark 16:17).

FAITH VERSUS FEELING

Faith is the prime essential when it comes to appropriating God's gifts. It is not surprising, therefore, that the Adversary would seek to undermine our faith by diverting our attention from the "faithfulness and worthiness" of the Giver to questions concerning the "validity" of the gift. He achieves this by raising doubts in our minds which may stem from our feelings or lack of feelings. How encouraging it is to realize that God's faithfulness is not determined by "how we feel" or "what we think" but by *what He has said.* God has said, "*Ask* and ye *shall* receive. *Believe* and these signs *shall* follow !" Faith never waits for "confirming feelings" but acts on the basis of God's eternal Word. Feelings fluctuate like the waves of the sea, but the Word of God is the solid rock on which our faith can firmly stand. *Faith is never passive; it al-*

ways acts ! In attitude, faith is "restful" but in action, it is "powerful." Praying in tongues has both a restful and powerful effect upon our lives because it is an active expression of our faith.

Basically, praying in tongues is something that we "do" not something that we "feel." We so pray because it is our privilege, and God in His faithfulness is worthy of our praise. His worthiness is not related to our feelings. We worship Him because He is worthy, not because He makes us "feel good." However, God has created us with the warm capacity to respond emotionally to His presence. We need not fear such feelings. Love is an emotion and God is love. Emotion is a powerful motivating force. Rather than "fear" our feelings, let us allow them to motivate us in God's way for God's will. We are not seeking a feeling, but a relationship with a Person. Once we have entered into this relationship, however, as in all personal relationships, we are going to have some feeling about it. Many of the graces of the Spirit have emotional overtones. Love, joy, peace, are greatly to be desired. How cold and gray Christianity would be without feeling ! The emotional overflow associated with our awareness of His infilling presence may vary in character. Some feel full of love; others joyful or peaceful. Still others have a warm sense of restfulness and rightness. When feelings are seen as a product rather than a source of our faith, they will assume a meaningful and rightful place in our Christian experience.

THE EXPRESSION OF FAITH

Faith acts ! But, how does it act ? The answer to this question is the key to your receiving the gift of God's Spirit in His fullness. The promise has already been given.

All that remains is for you to restfully but actively *take Him* at His Word.

Some time ago when we were located in Santa Barbara, California, it was our privilege to make the acquaintance of a visiting Canadian clergyman. God had placed a deep desire in his heart for a genuine Pentecostal experience that would enrich both his life and ministry. He had visited many "Pentecostal" meetings and had sensed the reality and presence of God's Spirit in. new ways to which he warmly responded. Unfortunately, he had observed on some occasions many things which he did not fully understand. Well-meaning individuals had violently shaken his head and shouted in his ear in their desire that he might receive the desire of his heart. Since he was conservative in nature, these experiences had been both discouraging and distressing. Some thoughtless individuals had even informed him that until his stiffnecked pride was broken, God had nothing for him. Little did they know of the times he had quietly slipped away broken in heart and spirit to be alone with God. There in the stillness of His presence He would fervently pray, often with tears, that God would fill his life to overflowing with His Spirit just as he saw recorded in the Book of Acts.

We seated ourselves on a stone bench in the middle of a small park around which was located a small neighborhood shopping center. After he had related the Lord's recent leading in his life concerning the Holy Spirit, we shared our own testimony with him. We began with Jesus as the focal point of the Father's love. We realized together that the Holy Spirit is God's only way to fill our lives with His Son. This is the purpose of a genuine Pentecostal experience. We agreed that we were not interested in some emotional crisis experience that would fade into the past. Rather, we were seeking a relationship with the Holy Spirit that would progressively reveal more of God's power and love through our lives.

We recognized further as we talked that he unconsciously had been seeking some "super-sensational" experience which God would sovereignly send forth somehow, some way, from the heavens above, as it were. As we compared the Gifts of God's Son and His Spirit we realized that both are usually entered into simply and sweetly by active faith in God's Word alone. Sensational experiences are the exception rather than the rule. Not everyone is knocked to the ground by a bright light and hears God's voice thunder from heaven as did the Apostle Paul !

Then we shared with him patterns of active faith from the Scriptures. Patterns which indicate that oftentimes man was required first to act in faith and obedience before God confirmed His word in experience. Moses had to pick up the rod and strike the rock before the life-giving refreshing waters flowed forth. There was nothing supernatural about striking the rock. It simply was obedient faith in action. Moses could have said, "Now, I want this to be 'all of God and none of me.' Lord, you pick up the rod and strike the rock !" If he had, he might have remained thirsty for a long time. It was not God's chosen way of active faith.

Peter saw His Lord walking on the water one stormy night on the Sea of Galilee. He desired to personally participate in this marvelous expression of God's power. If it was really of the Lord, Peter wanted this experience to be a part of his life. He cried out over the wind and waves, "Lord, if it be thou, bid me come unto thee on the water." And Jesus simply and quickly replied, "Come !"

Peter immediately responded to this word of the Lord

by a "leap of faith." It was a literal leap of faith, for in a moment's time Peter abandoned a lifetime of caution and fear of the sea and stepped forth upon the foaming waves. Not until he stepped out did the water become firm beneath his feet.

All went well as long as he kept his eyes on Jesus. But, as we are so prone to do sometimes, he began to doubt the reality of his experience. No longer were eyes of faith firmly fixed upon God's spoken word. That was when the "sinking feeling" came. Instantly Jesus caught and held him and simply said, "O thou of little faith wherefore didst thou doubt ?" I think Peter's faith was quickly restored by the touch of the Master's hand for they walked back to the boat . . . together. Only Peter stepped out, the rest waited in the boat. Only Peter walked on the water ! *Faith never passively waits; it always actively launches out.*

We then explained how our faith will express itself in appropriating the gift of God's Spirit in His fullness. Since he had prayed many times before that God would fill his life with the Holy Spirit, we suggested that this time he thank the Lord for answering prayer. After all, the Scripture clearly states, "Ask and ye shall receive !" As a further expression of his faith we indicated that it was his privilege to allow the infilling Spirit to direct through his lips a heavenly expression of praise and thanksgiving. "You mean all I have to do is just speak forth in faith in response to His presence ?" he inquired. We assured him that it was that simple and that we could bow our heads in prayer together right there for God was both ready and waiting.

Together we humbled ourselves in His presence. Together we confessed His faithfulness. Together we worshiped the Lord as His Spirit gave utterance ! After worshiping the Lord quietly for a time, he spoke these words,

"To think that God had led me 3,000 miles through all kinds of distressing experiences to a small park with the mountains on one side, the ocean on the other, and the blue sky above that I might learn that the fullness of God's Spirit is sweetly and restfully appropriated by a simple expression of child-like faith. Why, this is something I can take back to my people." And take it back he did! We just recently heard from him, and he joyfully related that some 50 young people in their summer camp had been filled with the Holy Spirit. Many had not even known Jesus as their Saviour, let alone as their Baptizer, before they came. In every gospel service there were conversions and by the end of the summer over 160 young people had accepted Jesus Christ. What a glorious chain reaction!

CHAPTER VIII

Release Your Faith

Let us personally express our desires at this point in the form of an inquiry. *How may I release my faith and find the reality of a personal, present-tense Pentecostal experience?*

Our first step is to humbly but confidently approach God as our loving and gracious Heavenly Father. We can then confess to Him both our need and His abundant supply. At a point in time we become prepared to specifically ask in faith for the fullness of His Holy Spirit. When we ask, we shall receive ! This is His promise. "God is not a man, that he should lie; neither the son of man, that he should repent: hath he said, and shall he not do it ? or hath he spoken, and shall he not make it good ?" (Numbers 23:19).

THE RESPONSE OF FAITH

By faith we breathe in the very life of God's Spirit until we are literally filled with His love. As we do, there will be an immediate awareness of His infilling presence. How we emotionally respond to this awareness of God is of secondary importance. How we actively and outwardly *respond* will be determined by our faith in God's Word. If we actually believe that the Spirit of God will now outwardly manifest His infilling presence just as He did throughout the Book of Acts, we will *actively* give Him our lips, our tongues, and our voices that He might direct

49

our praise heavenward in a divinely-given language. This is our "leap of faith" !

The infilling Spirit of worship will faithfully direct our praise as we boldly speak out in faith. At this point we must realize that faith will not express itself by our speaking in English or our native tongue. We are directing our speech at such times. Faith will turn our control over to the control of the Holy Spirit that we might speak in tongues as the Spirit gives us utterance.

Our native language is composed of sound which is broken up into syllables and words by our lips and tongue. The same is true when we pray in a heavenly language. *That* we speak is not supernatural. It is our voice, our lips, and our tongue, not God's. But, *what* we speak is supernatural for this is directed by God's Spirit. Faith, therefore, will surrender our faculties of speech to the Holy Spirit by actively lifting our voices and allowing Him to prompt our lips and tongues in the formulation of a heavenly expression.

HOW WE COOPERATE WITH
THE SPIRIT'S PROMPTINGS FOR PRAISE

The promptings of the Spirit may come in several different ways. Some sense an initial quivering of the lips producing a stammering sound. Rejoice in the knowledge that the infilling Holy Spirit is now faithfully prompting you to praise. Speak out the new sounds and syllables by moving your lips and tongue forcefully in faith.

Others feel an ill-defined urge to speak out from the abundance of their heart. Do so ! Don't worry what it "sounds like"; that's not up to you, but up to God. You give Him something to direct, and He will !

My wife and I prayed with a college student one Friday evening in our home. The Lord's presence was very real in a refreshing and restful way. Yet, our student friend was finding some difficulty in simply letting the Holy Spirit move through her life in a heavenly expression of praise. There were several questions which we first had to meet from God's Word. At last the young lady made a simple confession, "I am afraid it will sound silly." We assured her it would not sound silly to us or to God who warmly responds to even feeble expressions of our faith in His Word. We suggested that her statement sounded a little bit like pride. This she readily confessed and requested we pray together once more. As we did, she humbly spoke forth in faith and found to her joy a heavenly language hovering over her lips. The more she prayed the greater release did God give. Some months later it was her privilege to lead her own mother into the fullness of God's Spirit in like fashion.

Some sense inner promptings in the form of sounds or syllables in their minds. It is almost as if they know what the beginnings will sound like before they speak. Again, to speak forth in faith is all that is needed. To hold back for lack of some particular feeling is to cast doubt on God's Word. I recall a young woman praying at the church altar rail one evening until quite late. Whenever we would try to encourage her, she would always reply that she just didn't know how to yield to the Lord in spite of our careful instruction. Finally she said, "You know, I keep sensing strange syllables in my mind." We immediately encouraged her to follow the Spirit's leading and glorify God with what He had given her. She responded at once in faith, and the Lord faithfully gave her a lovely language in the Spirit with which to glorify Him.

Occasionally, God almost seems to move sovereignly in the lives of earnest seekers who are open to God's Word and way. It was our privilege to share the Scriptures concerning the Holy Spirit one evening in a prayer-and-share meeting in Los Angeles. A lady who was present had to leave before there was an opportunity for prayer. Later that night we learned that the Lord had awakened her with a heavenly language of praise upon her lips. Certainly God works in wondrous ways !

On the other extreme are those who seemingly have little feeling or obvious promptings as before mentioned. They do have faith, however, and the warm quiet evidence of God's infilling Spirit that faith always brings. This is sufficient. All that is necessary is to actively respond to this restful but very real presence of our faithful Lord. The venture of faith at such a time will always find vocal expression.

Some at this point would hesitate fearing that they would be "getting in the flesh." Or, as some have expressed it, "I am afraid it will just be me." Well in one sense who else would it be ? As in all of Christian experience, this is a cooperative venture in His grace. He desires to control not only our most unruly member but all that we are to glorify His Son.

FAITH VERSUS FEAR OF THE FLESH

For those who fear they will be "getting in the flesh," let us remember that it is "upon all flesh" that He is pouring out His Spirit. In other words, it is these earthly vessels of clay which He is filling with His Spirit. Let us not call common what the Spirit of the living God has divinely touched. By faith we are surrendering our most unruly member, these fleshy tongues of ours, to the purifying flame of God's Holy Spirit. Whatever sounds and syllables come streaming or even stammering forth have been prompted by the Spirit even though it is very much our voice, our lips, and our tongue which He is using.

For a sincere seeker to ask God in faith for the infilling of God's Spirit and the beautiful scriptural confirmation of a heavenly language and then receive something that was just of himself would be the coldest, hardest stone one could think of. *Yet, God's Word plainly, clearly, and emphatically declares that if we ask for bread, we will not get a stone!* How deceptive the Adversary is in cheating God's children out of their rightful heritage.

We prayed with a Methodist man in Houston, Texas, who claimed for years he had been carrying a "heavy stone" in spite of his pleas to God for the fullness of His Spirit. A word of wisdom flashed through our minds and we immediately replied, "No you haven't. You have been carrying bread all of these years but in doubt calling it a stone. No wonder you have received no strength and hope or sustenance, you have failed to partake of God's given gift !" His eyes brightened with understanding. Immediately, he lifted his head heavenward and opened his mouth in great expectation. There was a prompt overflow of praise in a lovely heavenly language. The next evening we visited his home and his wife was likewise filled. Jesus never fails !

Another man of the Christian Church had entered into the Spirit's fullness but doubted the stammerings of his initial praise in the Spirit. Someone had cautioned him about "getting in the flesh" and he had refrained from ever speaking forth again. When we met him he was greatly discouraged. He so longed for a heavenly release in prayer but was afraid it would just be himself. We counseled him from God's Word concerning the exercise of his faith. Again a word of wisdom crossed our minds and we explained how in a sense he had been given a "thousand dollar bill" but had never spent a cent because he was afraid it was a counterfeit. He realized the reflection this cast upon the Giver and promptly asked His forgiveness.

We then encouraged him to pray forth with great abandon knowing he could trust the faithfulness of the Holy Spirit without reservation. Immediately he broke forth in tongues, praising and magnifying God. With tears in his eyes he confessed how many times in his devotions, he had so wanted to praise God but was afraid. The next day in his newfound joy and faith he went forth and led a seeking soul to the Saviour. When we visited him a year later, he was still praising, witnessing, and "aglow with the Spirit." *God has not given us the spirit of fear but of faith !*

FAITH VERSUS DISCOURAGEMENT

Some are so discouraged from seeking God in faithless ways that they feel nothing except perhaps despair. How uplifting and enlightening God's way of active faith then becomes. We have seen this repeatedly in the lives of those who have become "chronic seekers." Once they see there is a part *they* are to play faithwise, their whole attitude changes. Upon experiencing God's faithfulness their usual response is, "Why, I could have simply yielded to the Holy Spirit in this way a long time ago if I had only known." God's way of childlike faith is so simple that Satan's greatest device of deception is to make us think there must be more to it. *Ask and respond in faith and you will most assuredly receive the Promise Given !*

I remember praying with a young man on one occasion who seemed very discouraged. I suggested that we talk together a little bit and that he share with us any questions which might be undermining his faith. He had only one question. It was the only thing between him and a heavenly release in God's Spirit. This was the question,

"Am I supposed to move my lips or will God ?" I suggested he lift his voice and move his lips and tongue in faith realizing that in this way he would be cooperating with the Holy Spirit's desire to direct his praise. His face brightened and immediately he raised his head heavenward in an attitude of expectation, opened his mouth, lifted his voice; and as he began to move his lips by faith, their immediately poured forth a beautiful language of praise. *God always confirms active faith in His Word !*

FAITH VERSUS FRUSTRATION

On another occasion we prayed with a lady in the home of one of my former students. Her prayer was so negative that we stopped her after a time. God can only respond to a prayer of faith, and vain repetitions begging God for a gift He has already given will be fruitless. *At such times God's Word is the only answer, for this is our only source of faith.*

We had sensed a spirit of restless frustration and soon discovered why. She had spent most of the previous night frantically begging God for His Holy Spirit until her throat was hoarse. We then suggested she lean back and relax in one of the overstuffed divans in the living room. Her lady friend sat beside her, and we began to share with them the quiet rest of faith. *Faith is firm but never feverish !* Paul reaches back into an Old Testament setting and brings forth a beautiful example in his discussion concerning the manifestation of tongues (1 Corinthians 14:21). "For with stammering lips and another tongue will he speak to this people. To whom he said, This is the rest wherewith ye may cause the weary to rest; and this is the refreshing: yet they would not hear" (Isaiah 28:-11,12).

The ways of God are restful and refreshing. Jesus said, "If any man thirst, let him come unto me . . . out of his belly (innermost being) will flow rivers of living water. This spake he . . . of the Holy Ghost . . ." (John 7:37-39).

After sensing and confessing His restful presence, we suggested we again lift our voices in praise as the Spirit would lead. At once she restfully began to softly sigh in the Spirit. I immediately witnessed to this sweet and gentle expression of her faith. She too recognized the deep inarticulate sighings as borne of the Spirit. We encouraged her to move her lips and tongue so as to form syllables, realizing in faith that these would be the promptings of God's Spirit. Immediately the beginnings of a new langauge began to find expression. Later in her own private devotions a greater liberty in spiritual praise was her reward for restful faith.

THE SUFFICIENCY OF SIMPLE FAITH

Perhaps the most discouraged person we ever prayed with was a Missionary Alliance man who was a returned missionary from one of the most primitive tribes in the world. His spiritual life had reached a low ebb and he was fast approaching what seemed to be a point of no return. The night he came to the church where we were speaking he was at the end of his rope. He later told the pastor that if God had not met him that night, he never would have darkened the door of the little church again.

He stayed at the end of the service; and after praying with several others, I asked if we could share with him in some way. He suggested we retire to one of the side rooms where we could talk. He promptly informed us that this was not a part of his background and he didn't understand it all. At first I thought he was going to argue, but he then proceeded to confess his great despair and

lack of spiritual direction. We ministered God's word of
assurance that the Holy Spirit wanted to fill his life with
the peace and power and purpose that he needed, right
then. He got down on his knees and requested we pray
without further delay. We prayed together that God would
meet the deep desires of his heart by His Spirit. Then he
began pleading with God to fill his life. We stopped his
prayer at this point and assured him that we need only
ask God once, then we are to act upon faith in His eternal
Word by lifting our voices in divinely directed praise. He
responded with a question, "Do you mean I am to pray
as you have been praying ?" (We had quietly been pray-
ing in tongues.) "Yes," we replied, "allow this to be your
expression of faith in God's infilling presence. Speak out
without reservation and don't stop regardless of doubts
or qualms. Trust Him. Prove His faithfulness." He began
softly without much conviction in his expression. But, he
didn't stop ! As he continued, his prayer became louder
and more fluent. Finally, there was such an exuberant ex-
pression of heavenly praise that he was even heard out in
the main sanctuary. I was no longer needed and made an
exit to the sanctuary. Sometime later an entirely different
man came out the door. Someone suggested we thank the
Lord for His faithfulness and the Spirit of praise swept
over him again as he stood in the aisle. The following
week was one of newfound power and praise, both day
and night. The Lord used him in saving lost souls, pray-
ing for the sick, and manifesting other spiritual gifts. It
was nothing short of a miracle. It is just as real in his life
today.

Now the interesting truth concerning faith in all of this
came to light in one of his remarks when we had fellow-
ship together afterwards. "You know," he said, "when
you suggested I simply step out in faith and begin pray-

ing in tongues, I thought it was about the most foolish thing I had ever done !" I realized then that he had no overwhelming "feeling" only a desperate faith that was willing to prove God in his hour of crisis. He saw no other way than God's way of faith and he took it. This was enough. *Simple faith in God's Word produces the miracle of the Spirit-filled life !* "Whoever *continues to believe* in me will have, as the Scripture says, rivers of living water *continuously flowing* from within him" (John 7:37, Williams' Translation).

THE PROMISING PATHWAY OF PROGRESSIVE FAITH

One of the most beautiful illustrations of God's desire to reward our active faith occurred while we were teaching in a Christian College on the West Coast. One of our college students had come to our home for prayer concerning a physical need; and in the course of our fellowship together, God had filled her with His Spirit. She returned home and told her mother that God had filled "the hole in her heart" with Himself.

In the fall, her mother came by our home for fellowship and prayer. She was a deeply spiritual person and had had experiences in the Lord where the Holy Spirit had literally bathed her with His presence almost beyond her human capacity. She was an experienced soul-winner and a faithful intercessor in prayer. She was certain that her life had been filled with God's Spirit but was desirous for the privilege to pray with the Spirit in devotional tongues. She was willing for all that God might have for her.

After spending some time in God's Word together, we prayed that the infilling Holy Spirit might overflow her life in a heavenly language of praise. I was almost expecting a mighty rushing wind to sweep down upon such

an obvious saint of the Lord, to be followed by an ex-
uberant flow of God's praise ! This is not what happened.
In fact, nothing happened. We encouraged her to step
forth in faith and lift her voice to God in praise. After
a moment I heard one little sound that sounded somewhat
like "uhh." I was hardly prepared for such a feeble effort
in faith, but I encouraged her in the fact that this was her
initial step in yielding to the Holy Spirit. I ministered the
word of faith and prayed again. This time there were
several slow little syllables, but that was all. I realized she
was probably waiting for some sensational experience as
she had experienced before. I cautioned her about looking
to feelings. She readily responded for she had used the
same faith promises many times when dealing with indi-
viduals about the Gift of God's Son.

We prayed again and this time there were a couple of
different little syllables which quickly trailed off into noth-
ing. I then shared with her an account which we had read
in John E. Stiles book, *The Gift of the Holy Spirit.* At the
close of one of his services, he briefly prayed for a woman
who had come for the infilling of the Holy Spirit. She im-
mediately lifted her voice in fervent praise, but she re-
peatedly expressed only one little syllable. It must have
sounded like stammering. As he watched amazed at such
a child-like expression of faith, the Lord gave him a vision
of a little stalk-like shoot which was inching its way up-
ward everytime she would toss back to heaven her one
God-given syllable. Presently, there were two such syl-
lables which she now used joyfully, not doubting or ques-
tioning, but delighted with her newfound expression of
praise, simple though it was. A little branch appeared on
the stalk as the new syllable found expression. Soon there
were other syllables and branches, until after a time she
was fluently speaking in a heavenly language and his vis-

ion portrayed a beautiful symmetrical tree. He asked the
Lord to reveal to him the meaning of the vision which he
could still see. God brought to his mind the account of the
hornets which the Lord promised He would use to drive
back the Canaanites as the Children of Israel moved into
the Promised Land. The hornets didn't move them back
all at one time, but little by little at a sufficient rate which
would allow the Israelites to accompish their possession of
the land. "By little and little I will drive them out from
before thee, until thou be increased, and inherit the land"
(Exodus 23:30). The application the Lord then made is
obvious. The more the lady was possessing by faith and
actively expressing, the more God was giving little by
little, until the promise was fully possessed. I explained the
simple truth of this story to the mother of our student.
"The more we use of what God gives; the more will He
give." Not everyone possesses the land all at once. Some
do, but others come by the way of faith, little by little.
The result is the same ! We explained to her that we never
become discouraged when counseling and praying with
those who move slowly. To see and to learn the principle
of active faith is well worth the time.

We prayed again, and this time there was a break-
through of several different but divinely given words of
praise. There was an immediate witness in all of our hearts
concerning God's faithfulness. The hour was now late,
and I suggested that she retire and in the privacy of her
own devotions gain a further release in prayer.

In the morning before she left for home, she told us that
she awoke in the night and had sensed these words turn-
ing over in her mind and that she knew that it was real.
Then she left. Later that day we received a long distance
phone call from her relating the rest of the story. As she
was driving along, she decided she would pray in her new

found language of praise. She began to pray and to sing. And, to her utter amazement, not only was God giving her heavenly words but a beautiful melody as well. In fact, she was so enraptured by this time in worshipping God that when the Greyhound bus she was following took the wrong turn, she went right along with it for several miles before realizing she had missed the way. Obviously, however, she had not missed the "heavenly way." We have heard from her many times since, and she has been so grateful to the Lord for enriching her devotional and prayer life in such a meaningful way.

The lesson we learn from this story, of course, is to pursue the pathway of promise with active faith. *We are not to doubt or question God's way but to walk in it.* It is a wonderful way, and He beckons to us now to "come away with Him."

OUR PERSONAL TESTIMONY

It would be difficult to conclude this chapter without sharing with you our own testimony. It was during the year of 1955 that God began to move in our lives in new ways. We were located in Houston, Texas. Our family then was composed of three children; I was an instructor in Anatomy at Baylor University College of Medicine. We were settled in our new home and established in an independent Bible-centered church. I was teaching a high-school Sunday-school class, serving on the Board of Deacons, and active in the Men's Missionary Fellowship.

From all outward appearances we should have been very satisfied and contented. The Lord, however, searches out the hearts of men, and within me He found a heart that was reaching out for a dimension that was missing. I was engaged in doing many right things. I read many right books and prayed many right prayers. The Lord, however, was showing me that one's life could be very "right" but also very "unreal." It is possible to be coldly correct and miss the warm reality of the Lord's manifest presence that characterized the early New Testament Church.

As I read the Book of Acts, I discovered that here were men full of faith, wisdom, power and joy. Their secret seemed to be related to the fullness of the Spirit, for repeatedly I found the above realities linked with the little phrase "and full of the Holy Ghost" (Acts 6:3,5,8; 13:52). I knew I was indwelt by His Spirit, but I longed for His fullness in a way that would align my life with theirs. I was not content to read about something that was real some 2,000 years ago; I wanted to experience it now.

The Lord never mocks the honest heart nor frustrates the sincere seeker. I was no exception. Through His Word, the Holy Spirit deepened my desire to know more of the beauty and power of Jesus Christ, and He planted and nurtured within me a sense of great expectation. Finally, one Friday morning I came to the end of myself and told the Lord in desperation I could not go on without this hunger for Himself finding fulfillment. God answered that prayer the same day.

I was in the kitchen preparing the children's lunch following a time of earnest prayer when a very real and very warm awareness of His great love for me seemed to descend from the heaven above. I remember I couldn't understand why He should love me so, but He did anyway! I also found I did not have words to express my deep love for Him in return. At that point I stepped into the hallway and allowed the infilling Holy Spirit to magnify God through me in a divinely-directed way just as I had read they did in the Book of Acts when the Promise of the Father was possessed by faith. They were all filled with the Holy Spirit and magnified God in other tongues. God had answered my prayer and a whole new dimension in the Spirit-filled life began to unfold progressively.

The Lord has always led my wife and me together in our Christian experience, and we were not surprised, therefore, for God to lead her into the infilling reality of the Holy Spirit in the same wonderful way a short time later.

Since that time we have discovered that the deep desires of our hearts for the fullness of God's Spirit are also the desires of hungry hearts everywhere. Furthermore, God is faithfully pouring out His Spirit upon every life that reaches out for Him in faith. He is no respector of persons and He stands ready to answer your prayer even now. In fact, if you will pray in faith that the Holy Spirit will honor God's Word in your life as we share His Word with you, you will receive the Holy Spirit in His fullness before you close the pages of this chapter. *This is His promise !*

YOU MAY RECEIVE HIM NOW

Many additional accounts could be given of God's faithfulness to those who dare to believe His Word. If you sense a stirring in your heart in response to all that you have read, *pause just now and ask God to deepen your desire for more of Him.*

Only the Spirit of God can satisfy the deep desires that He has given us for Jesus. If you ask Him to fill your life just now, He will. He promised ! "Ask, and ye shall receive." Why don't you ask Him right now ? *He is waiting for you.*

Now *confess* to the Lord that you *believe* His Word. Thank Him for filling your life with His blessed Holy Spirit. Rejoice in the full awareness of His personal presence.

As an *active expression of your faith* in the fact that the

Holy Spirit now fills your being, open your mouth, lift your voice, and move your lips and tongue in cooperation with the prompting of the Holy Spirit. Do not stop, but allow a steady stream of praise to ascend heavenward as you now magnify God in a heavenly language. The more you use, the more God will give. He cannot fail ! As you gain an increased liberty in praise, remember that your prayer is as a sweet incense, an acceptable sacrifice, well-pleasing to God.

We rejoice with you in the Lord. Bless His wonderful name !

CHAPTER IX

Prayer in the Spirit

Being filled with the Holy Spirit opens up a whole new dimension in your Christian life. Your initial experience is but the *beginning* of an exciting and wonderful adventure in the Lord. You have launched out into the life abundant. As you mature in your experience, it need never lose its freshness. *The Holy Spirit is the never-failing Spirit of hope and expectation.*

This does not mean that there will not be trials and even persecution. In fact, the power of Satan will be felt as never before. But, you have a heavenly resource in the Holy Spirit who by faith will release the power, wisdom, and love of Christ through your life each day.

Therefore, begin each day by giving the day back to God and fully committing yourself to the Holy Spirit who desires to equip, teach, and use you for His glory. Expect something new from God each day *for* you; that *through* you, He may draw others to Himself.

Faith is characterized by its object. The object of our faith is a great God. Great faith will have great expectations ! Begin to believe for God's daily working in your life in ways that will be as wonderful and amazing as He is. "Eye hath not seen, nor ear heard, neither have entered into the heart of man, the things which God hath prepared for them that love him. But God hath revealed them unto us by His Spirit" (1 Corinthians 2:9,10). "The things" referred to in the above passage are the "all things" which pertain to Jesus which the Holy Spirit will show unto us (John 16:15). In other words Jesus is going to become progressively more real to you than He has ever been before. You will know more and more of *His* love and of *His* power and of *His* wisdom in your life ! This is what it means to live a Spirit-filled life. "If we live in the Spirit, let us also walk in the Spirit" (Galatians 5:25). The spiritual walk of the Christian has direction. We are going somewhere. The "somewhere" is really "someone" . . . Jesus Christ !

Let us see how the Holy Spirit desires to bring life to Christian experience in the areas of prayer, Bible study and witness. We will begin with prayer.

I remember a pastor once exclaiming right after receiving the fullness of God's Spirit in praise, "Why, prayer won't be a chore anymore !" He was absolutely right. The Holy Spirit is the Spirit of prayer. When we by faith close ourself off to pray "with God's Spirit," we are entering into a most meaningful experience. There is indeed a refreshing and a release. *Prayer should be as alive as is the God to whom we pray.* One of the most deadening things in Christian experience is to "say prayers" instead of talking to God.

I can remember during "circle prayers" awaiting my turn and carefully rehearsing what and how I was going to pray. Occasionally, someone else would "steal" my prayer before my turn came, and I would be left high and dry and at a loss for words. I somehow suspect that my part of the prayer circle was about as satisfactory to God as it was empty for me. I have since discovered that I was not alone in my frustration, although this is really of little comfort. How hollow our prayers can sometimes be. It is the desire of the Holy Spirit to fill our lives with praise and prayer. He neither slumbers nor sleeps and prays without ceasing. If we are filled with God's Spirit, we are filled with never-failing prayer. By faith we can "tune in" to the Spirit of prayer and "with Him" lift heaven-ward our confessions, intercessions, petitions and praise. No wonder Paul encourages us to pray "with our spirit as moved by His spirit" (1 Corinthians 14:15, Amplified New Testament and Wuest's Expanded Translation). This truth is further reinforced in Ephesians 6:18 and Jude 20 where we are admonished to pray "in, by means of, through" the Holy Spirit that we might stand strong and be built up in the most holy faith (various translations).

Praying in tongues and with our understanding is an active expression of *a living faith in a living God.* One of the most exciting experiences of the Spirit-filled life is that God really does answer prayer. To *say* it is one thing; to *see* it is another. If we say it in faith, we will see it in life . . . our life !

I recall the remark of a professional colleague of mine who just recently has been filled with the Holy Spirit. A brush fire was threatening the home of a mutual friend early one Sunday afternoon. An appeal for prayer was made, and we all responded by seeking God's protection for their home. The flames were checked and their home was saved. My colleague later told us of their prayer experience at the time. They had taken time out from the activities of Sunday dinner and had prayed an earnest but short prayer for God's intervention. He immediately felt that God had heard and would act accordingly. They rejoiced but were not surprised to learn of the outcome. "It's a funny thing," he said, "but before being filled with God's Spirit, I never would have had that kind of faith." Jesus is the Author and Finisher of our faith (Hebrews 12:2). The Holy Spirit of faith simply makes Him more real to us.

OUR PRAYER OF PRAISE

There are several different expressions to prayer. We have already mentioned the purpose and power in praise. *Praise is a very positive expression of our faith !* It should be a continual part of our daily experience. Our last thoughts at night and our first thoughts in the morning should be those of praise to God. As a compass needle immediately swings to the north when distracting forces are removed so should our minds go fleeting back to God in worship all throughout the day as we move from one mental task to another. A great deal of God's power can quickly be compressed into our lives as periodically we lift our voices audibly or inaudibly as the occasion may allow to Him in divinely-directed praise. There is great edifying power in praying in tongues all throughout the day. Here is one way we can repeatedly "tune in" to the unceasing Spirit of praise who faithfully fills our lives with His presence.

Some time ago we received a letter from a lady and her husband whom it had been our privilege to lead into the fullness of the Holy Spirit. She was describing the new joy that God had brought to their lives and how Thanksgiving Day had been the most wonderful Thanksgiving they had ever spent together.

Then she shared something I will never forget. "Do you notice," she said, "that we seem to be saying, 'Praise God' more since we 'received.' The words 'Praise God' flow so easily from our lips, and these words seem to be definitely connected with our heart. Anyway, I seem to get a little 'pang' when I say it."

This really touched my heart. In fact, it brings tears to my eyes just to think about it again. I know what she was talking about ! The Holy Spirit has a way of linking our hearts with Jesus when we praise Him that brings a thrill to this earthly life of ours. To know the touch of Jesus is to be spoiled for anything else as far as real joy in this world is concerned. How apart from His Spirit could we ever praise Him as we should !

Praising God in tongues can become a sensitive thermometer for the Spirit-filled Christian. Only a life filled with God will continually want to praise Him. Conversely, one of the first dimensions to go in a life where the Holy Spirit has been grieved will be the desire to praise God. The Spirit of worship has been quenched. Our communion with the Holy Spirit around the praise-worthiness of God's Son has been broken. Even the slightest sin unconfessed will dampen our desire to praise the Lord.

I have found in my own life that this is one of the ways the Holy Spirit will most quickly and specifically bring to my attention some sin that needs to be confessed. It is impossible to praise God in tongues and be irritated at one's children at the same time. God has a way of desiring our praise in the midst of most "earthy" situations. *Any attitude of heart or mind which robs God of the praise He deserves is sin.* As soon as it is confessed in faith, our communion with the Holy Spirit in Christ is restored. So is our joy and peace in the Lord. How worthy He is of our praise !

OUR PRAYER OF CONFESSION

We now rather naturally come to another expression of prayer, that of confession. *Confession in prayer must always be of a twofold nature, negative and positive.* "Negatively" we confess our sins, mistakes, missteps, imperfections, and great need. We readily confess all that we are not. And, in ourselves, we are nothing ! Then in faith and with rejoicing we "positively" confess our Saviour, His

forgiveness, His perfection, and our righteousness in Him.
We readily confess all that He is. And, in Him we have
everything !

Satan is very subtle and will always try to limit our
confession to repeated negatives. Sometimes he will point
an accusing finger at some defect in our life and through
continual condemnation drive us to despair and discour-
agement. Our testimony at such a time is completely neu-
tralized, and God's will for our lives frustrated. This is
one way Satan endeavors to undermine our witness for
Christ. *We should be prepared to overcome such an evil
Spirit of despair by actively presenting a positive confes-
sion of our faith.*

I remember an occasion in our own lives that required
just such an expression of our faith before the darkness of
discouragement was defeated. I had been invited to speak
at a Christian Advance meeting in Riverside, California.
The weather was hot and by the late afternoon our entire
family was tired and a little on the edgy side. To make
matters worse we lost our way, and I was growing fearful
that we might be late. As time progressed, I became more
irritable within and sharp-spoken without. Before long,
however, the Holy Spirit faithfully impressed me how
grievous this was to the Lord. We no sooner had con-
fessed our failure than this barbed thought flashed through
our minds, "How could we stand before an audience that
evening and minister the peace and joy of the Lord when
our own lives had been such an obvious contradiction."
My heart sank in despair and a fear bordering on inner
panic overwhelmed me. God's faithful Spirit then brought
a word of hope to my remembrance. Had God not said,
"That if we confess our sins, He would be faithful and
just to forgive us our sins and *cleanse us from all un-
righteousness"?* This meant simply that we would again

be clean and fit vessels for God's Spirit to fill. God said so ! We immediately made this positive confession with our full understanding quickened by the Holy Spirit. As a further expression of our faith we moved on into devotional tongues allowing this release to be a means of "washing from our life" the inner tensions and confusion. As the Holy Spirit used this means of grace to edify our lives, an awareness of His peace brought a quietness to our troubled souls.

That night, God's hand of evident blessing was upon His Word as we ministered to hungry hearts. In a most encouraging way God confirmed to us again the overcoming power which He brings to a positive confession of our faith. *The Holy Spirit will always honor a positive confession of God's Word !* If we confess anything less than this, the Spirit is grieved and we quench His work and witness in our lives.

OUR PRAYER OF INTERCESSION

Another dimension in our prayer is related to intercession. Here, by faith we allow the Holy Spirit to *identify* ourselves with a personal need and at the same time to *identify* ourselves with the divine supply which is in the Lord Jesus. *The intercessory prayer of faith bridges heaven and earth on the behalf of someone that God has laid upon our hearts. We become God's link of love.* Jesus was and is an intercessor. If we are to become like Him, we too will allow the Spirit of intercession to move us to prayer.

Praying in tongues gives intercessory prayer a powerful dimension. Perhaps at no other time do we more keenly feel the limitations of our understanding. The force of our prayer is weakened by the fact that we do not know how to pray as we ought. How good of God to provide a way which bypasses the limitations of our minds and of our speech. We know that divinely-expressed intercession will always be in keeping with God's divine purposes. This provides a real safeguard for our prayers and allows our faith to find full expression without reservations concerning His will.

How easy it is for us sometimes to program somebody else's life. We begin to project into our prayer what we think would be God's will for their lives. Just recently we have seen the Lord answer our prayers for someone in a most unusual way. It was something we never would have anticipated. God very clearly showed us the danger of limiting Him by tending to rely upon our understanding alone. God works in ways which to man are mysterious. *Praying in tongues is one way that the mysteries of God can be spoken without passing through the restricting filter of our minds.*

OUR PRAYERS OF PETITION

Lastly, let us consider our prayers of petition. Jesus said that if we would ask anything in His name He would do it that the Father would be glorified in the Son (John 14:13). The "anything" is qualified in a twofold way. First of all, *we must present the name of Jesus with our petition.* That name represents who He is and what He has accomplished for us. Secondly, *what we ask for must be so related to Jesus that it will bring glory to the Father.* In other words, everything in our lives whether large or small, earthly or heavenly, people, places, or things, is to revolve around God's Son. *Every prayer must place Jesus in its center !* If we are sure of this, then we can ask anything in all confidence.

Prayers should never become commonplace. We may pray in common places but always with an awareness that God is near and hears every word. Some time ago my wife attended a small prayer-and-share group in Tulsa, Oklahoma. Following the prayer time one of the ladies approached my wife and said, "As you were praying I saw Jesus standing beside you with His hand upon your head." When she shared this with me, I couldn't help but think that God in His grace sometimes pushes back the curtains of this earthly life of ours just enough for us to see how very close He really is. Many of the prayers offered that night have already been answered. God really does answer prayer ! *To be filled with the Spirit is to be filled with prayer !*

CHAPTER X

The Spirit and God's Word

"In the beginning was the Word and the Word was with God, and the Word was God . . . And the Word was made flesh, and dwelt among us, (and we beheld his glory, the glory as of the only begotten of the Father), full of grace and truth" (John 1:1,14).

In the written Word of God is revealed the living Word of God, the Lord Jesus Christ. *He is the integrating theme of Holy Scripture.* God's full will centers in His Son, and this truth is progressively revealed as one moves from Genesis to Revelation. We become an integral part of God's holy will when we become identified with His Son. We become an integral part of God's holy way when we become identified with His Spirit. It is in God's Word that we discover the meaning of His will and way for our lives.

One of the first things that newly Spirit-filled believers discover is that the Word of God has suddenly become alive for them in a new way. Many have been the times that we have been amazed at the fresh insights from God's Word that have been shared with us by college students who had recently come to know the fullness of the Holy Spirit in their lives. This should not be surprising, however, for it is the purpose of the Holy Spirit to *illuminate* our understanding of God's Word (1 Corinthians 2).

It is most interesting when we become aware that the books of the New Testament were written by Spirit-filled believers to Spirit-filled believers. The authors of the Epistles took for granted that the recipients of their divinely-inspired letters had already received both the gifts of God's Son and His Spirit. Pentecostal experience was the rule not the exception. A greater appreciation and understanding of the Scriptures are obtained when we realize that the grand themes of the Epistles find expression in our lives through the spiritual fruit and gifts. *The Word of God is the raw material the Holy Spirit uses to build Christ into our lives. As we live in the Word, the life of the Word becomes ours !*

The other morning I awoke with three words repeatedly going through my mind. They were these: informed, transformed, and conformed. As I pondered what significance the Holy Spirit would attach to this, the following thoughts began to develop. First of all, before we can become *conformed* into the image of Christ, we must willingly and faithfully expose our minds to His. The mind of God is revealed in His Word. Therefore, we must consistently expose ourselves to the Holy Scriptures. In this way we become Christ-*informed*. As we do, the Holy Spirit will *transform* and renew our minds like unto His (Romans 12:2). We will progressively begin to think His thoughts rather than our thoughts. We will become more and more Christ-minded. Now, our thoughts determine what we are, what we say and what we do. Therefore, to the extent that we think as Jesus thinks, we will be, say and do as Jesus is, says and does. In other words, we will become *conformed* into His image ! How supremely important is God's Word for your life and mine.

How might one practically and personally begin to "search the Scriptures daily" ? First of all, it is suggested that one obtain a King James Bible with large print and wide margins. A small plastic ruler and a micropoint ball

pen will provide the means for underlining pertinent pas-
sages and personalizing them with marginal notes. A good
concordance, Bible dictionary, and single volume com-
mentary are also recommended. To this should be added
a modern version of the Bible for added accuracy and
freshness. Spend some time in a Bible bookstore finding
the volumes which are most readable and suited to your
personal preferences.

One might begin with the Gospel of John and the Book
of Acts and follow the events preceding and following
Pentecost. Here are the reactions of people just like you
and me as they approach and enter into this new adven-
ture of the Spirit-filled life. Try to imagine how you would
have felt and acted if you had been there. *You will soon
be reliving in your life now, much of what you read in
their lives then.* God's will and way have never changed !

Paul's epistle to the Colossians is a beautiful and power-
ful portrayal of the preeminence and centrality of the Lord
Jesus Christ. We see Him pictured as "Lord of all." We
are "complete in Him," and now the Holy Spirit wants to
increasingly make Him "complete in us." This is how He
becomes Lord of our life !

The full beauty and power of Christ can only be found
in the Church or body of believers. In Paul's letter to the
Ephesians, we see the part we are to play in the ministry
of the Church. The spiritual gifts and graces are the means
of equipping our lives for the edification of the Church.
We will have more to say concerning this in the next
section.

Even in the Old Testament, spiritual truth will find
expansion when it is recast into the words, works and per-
son of Christ. For example, the Psalmist declares that the
godly man's "delight is in the law of the Lord; and in his
law doth he meditate day and night" (Psalm 1:2). The

Spirit-filled Christian would recognize the added significance this has for him when he realizes that the law was God's Word and that Jesus is the living Word and fulfillment of the law. To substitute Jesus for the word "law" lends a beauty to the passage which enhances our understanding. "The godly man's delight is in Jesus, and in Him doth he meditate day and night."

Sometimes it is meaningful to personalize spiritual *principles* and *promises* by restating the passage in the margin and inserting the pronoun "I" or "me". In this way, for instance, the spiritual principles in God's promises to Israel can become ours personally. Isaiah 43:1,2 declares, "Fear not: for I have redeemed thee, I have called thee by thy name; thou art mine. When thou passest through the waters, I will be with thee; and through the rivers, they shall not overflow thee . . ." How powerfully personal this becomes when in the margin we write, "I am not to fear. Christ has redeemed me. I have been called by name. I am His. He is with me. I shall not be overwhelmed."

The Holy Spirit will always honor a positive confession of God's Word in faith. This is the means by which His will *for* our lives becomes real *in* our lives. The more we expose ourselves to God's Word, the greater becomes our faith in God's Word (Romans 10:17). Through it the Holy Spirit brings peace and power and sustained purpose to our lives. Through the *written Word* the Holy Spirit imparts the *Living Word* to our lives. If we do not honor the place of the Holy Scriptures in our daily experience, we quickly grieve God's Spirit in us and frustrate His will for us. It is the deep desire of the Holy Spirit to make God's living word our daily life. Jesus said, "I am the bread of life." May we quickly reply, "Give us this day our daily bread."

To be filled with the Spirit is to be filled with God's Holy Word !

CHAPTER XI

The Spirit and Our Witness

The primary purpose of our Pentecostal experience is for power to witness to others of Jesus Christ. The word "witness" means to testify or furnish evidence of something we have seen, heard or directly experienced. The Holy Spirit first makes Jesus Christ real to us in personal experience. He then enables us to furnish evidence of our living Lord to others by manifesting His life through us in thought, word and deed. The fruit and gifts of the Spirit are the means by which others "see and hear" Christ in us. From this we can quickly see that the word "witness" means far more than passing out tracts or inviting someone to church, although on occasion both of these activities may be involved.

To live is to witness ! It is not a matter of *whether* we are going to be a witness or not, but rather *what* we are going to be witnesses of and *how* effective that witness will be. The purpose of the Holy Spirit in our lives is that we may be a continual daily witness for Jesus Christ.

Witnessing for our Lord should be as real and natural as is our life. However, wherever, or whenever someone comes into our daily lives, they should encounter Jesus Christ. The rules for witnessing are basically very simple. *Live Christ and love others !* The way that love is expressed may be soft and gentle, or swift and powerful. Both expressions are found in principle and practice throughout the Epistles and the Book of Acts. The Holy Spirit sometimes moves powerfully as a mighty rushing wind, and oftentimes gently as a circling dove about to alight. Such too was the life of Christ. In gentle love He gathered the little children around Him. In great power He evidenced His authority by setting free those who were possessed by Satan's power.

There is no greater privilege given to man than that of sharing the Gifts of God's Son and His Spirit with others. As we give ourselves and each day back to God, may we pray that He will bring someone with a prepared and open heart across our path. May we be sufficiently sensitive to God and others to recognize the encounter when it comes. And, come they will for God will divinely order our lives to reach others if we expectantly ask Him to do so.

We should continually be alert all throughout each day for God may bring opportunities our way when and where we least expect them. Many have been the times that we have found ourselves sharing God's Word in situations we could never have anticipated. There is real adventure in the Christian life. God works in both marvelous and amazing ways to accomplish His will. If we ask God to prove Himself in our desire to be a Spirit-filled witness, He will take us at our word. You may find yourself in strange places sharing with strange people at strange times; but one thing sure, you will never be bored. *The Holy Spirit is one sure cure for boredom !* Life will never be the same for the Spirit-filled believer. Every Christian should be motivated by this overwhelming sense of divine destiny.

When opportunities come to share God's Son and His Spirit with interested inquirers, let us be careful that *this* is what we share. We can tell them how God has confirmed His Word to us personally. We *know* God's Son ! We *know* God's Spirit ! It is our desire to introduce them to those whom we know and love. The best way to do this is to share how real God has made His Word to us in everyday life. We have to bring heaven to earth, for this is where they are.

This may involve time and patience. We reach over to others by the bridge of love. Jesus said, "Greater love hath no man than this that a man lay down his life for his friends." What is our life ? Is it not composed of our time, energy, interests, and desires ? *Love will give life, ours for others !* As we so give of ourselves as He gave of Himself, there will come a time when the one whom God has loved through us will desire to enter into God's gifts. Our part then is to minister the Word of God in great faith and power. The Holy Spirit will always honor God's Word. This He will do regardless of time, place, or circumstance ! *Real faith will never limit God.*

A short time ago it was our privilege to visit some Spirit-filled Episcopalian friends of ours in a nearby town. They told us of a young friend of theirs with whom they had shared their testimony. He was planning on entering the ministry and currently was employed as a television clown on a local children's program. The Sunday of our departure our friends called and inquired if we would like to meet the young man. He had a television program in the afternoon and was going to the church afterwards to perform for the children at an ice-cream social. Following this, there were further commitments for the evening. There was the possibility, however, that we could visit with him for a little while between afternoon and evening commitments.

We arrived at the church social while he was in the midst of his performance with the children. Following this, he and my friend slipped away to the rector's study where we could visit together for a time. He removed his wig and sat down. He was still dressed in his clown suit and wearing makeup in colorful patterns. It was a strange combination of events that had brought us all together under such unusual circumstances.

We shared together of the Lord's leading in all of our lives and of our mutual desire for His full will and power in each of us. I told him of the Holy Spirit's moving among the Episcopalians we had known on the West Coast, and how our own lives had been changed by God's Spirit. We carefully related our experience to God's Word and God's Son. He warmly responded to all that we said and requested that we might pray with him that he too might know the fullness of the Holy Spirit in his life. As we all bowed our heads in worship, we prayed that God would honor the faith in his heart and fill him with an overflowing Spirit of praise. He immediately began to worship God in a heavenly language of love. Just as we were through, the door opened and his friend arrived to take him to his next appointment.

I couldn't help but think afterwards of how marvelously the eternal God can divinely order the events of time to accomplish His purposes. Furthermore, we realized as never before that God is not limited by outward appearances or circumstances. *God will meet a searching soul anywhere or anytime his faith reaches out to embrace the promises of His Word.*

It is also comforting to know that God is not honoring us with all our limitations but the in-living Christ and His out-spoken Word. How wise it is for us to remember from time to time that we cannot convert anyone to Christ or fill anyone with God's Spirit. This is the work and responsibility of God alone. Our part is to show open-hearted and ready-minded people how to exercise their faith in God's Word so they may receive God's gifts.

The scriptural pattern for active faith is simple and sure. *"Believe* in thine heart and *confess* with thy mouth." The greatest problem is convincing people from the Scripture that the pattern is really this simple . . . There is really nothing more to do, God has done everything else !

Our witness should always be very Christ-centered and firmly grounded in God's Word. Begin with Jesus and end with Jesus. Relate every experience to God's Word. God always confirms His Word in experience; therefore the two must go hand-in-hand. Satan can cause us to doubt our experiences if we don't first find them firmly rooted in God's Word. Our experience will be only as strong as our faith is firm !

Many move into the Gifts of God's Son and His Spirit and then do not move on as they should because the purpose and support from the Scriptures is lacking. It is not enough to lead others into God's gifts alone. The meaning of the gifts must be grounded in the Word and related to God's purpose for their lives.

Just recently it was our privilege to visit for several hours with a Lutheran pastor on the Gulf Coast. It was one of those encounters which God brings into our lives for mutual profit. We shared our testimony with him and he shared his with us. As his story unfolded, we learned that he had attended a meeting in the spring where an account of the Holy Spirit's move in the historic churches was given. He went to a side room for prayer and counsel afterwards. He honestly told the Lord that he wanted anything God had for him if through it he might better serve and worship God. Someone showed him the passage in Luke Eleven which promises that if we ask we shall receive. He then in faith lifted his voice and spoke forth in a heavenly language of sustained praise as the infilling Spirit gave utterance. Some time later an elderly little lady approached him and indicated she had seen in vision a white mantle which overshadowed him as he prayed.

In spite of such almost sensational experiences, he later began to question the validity of what had happened. In fact, he finally dismissed his experience as nothing more than autosuggestion. The Lord, however, over the next few months kept bringing the matter to his attention through his reading and contacts with ministerial colleagues. A seminary professor cautioned him about depreciating any gift God might give in response to a sincere prayer of faith based on God's Word and for His glory. He also discovered that one of his colleagues had just recently entered into the same experience in the Holy Spirit. Some of this had happened just prior to our visit with him. We then shared with him how God had meaningfully related our own personal experience in the Holy Spirit to His Word and to His Son.

We visited together for sometime encouraging one another in the faith. As we parted, we both confessed God's utter faithfulness and our deep desire to worship and serve Him with every means that God's Spirit makes available to us. Devotional tongues was seen as a meaningful gift to edify us and glorify God. *True spiritual experiences will always appear both "right" and "real" when seen in the light of God's Word.*

Once again the Lord impressed upon me the necessity of grounding everything in His Holy Word. *God's Spirit will always honor God's Word to glorify God's Son.* This He will do experimentally in your life and mine. Our experience is real because God's Word is real. The purpose of the Holy Spirit is to confirm the living Word of God in our lives. This is our witness !

To be filled with the Holy Spirit is to be filled with power to witness !

CHAPTER XII

Fellowship in the Spirit

The Greek New Testament word translated "fellowship" means sharing a common interest. When applied to Christian fellowship, the common interest around which we are united is a person. That Person is Jesus Christ! Faith in Christ as our Lord and Saviour will be the basis for our future fellowship together in heaven and should be the only basis for our fellowship together here on earth.

The more real Jesus becomes in and through our lives, the more real our fellowship with fellow believers becomes! If we are united to Christ, we are united to one another. He is our basis for fellowship. The Holy Spirit is the Spirit of unity because He is the one who relates us to Jesus. One of the most striking and amazing characteristics of this latter-day outpouring of the Holy Spirit has been the bond of love for one another which marks real Spirit-filled believers. This Spirit of love cuts across all the barriers of peripheral doctrine and practice and links us together around Christ alone. The unifying power of the Holy Spirit is a most marvelous thing to behold and experience. "Behold how good and how pleasant it is for brethren to dwell together in unity! It is like precious ointment upon the head . . . and the dew that descended upon the mountains," says the Psalmist (Psalm 133). What beautiful pictures of the Holy Spirit's work in building up Christ's body, the living Church.

The simplest expression of the Church is where two or

three are gathered together in Jesus' name. He has promised to be there in the midst of them (Matthew 18:20). Actually, it is only through the Body of Christ or Fellowship of Believers that God's *full* glory can be manifested to the world. It is only through the fellowship of *many* believers that God's manifold expressions of beauty and power can be *fully* revealed. We each have an integral part of that power and beauty through the gifts and graces, but we need one another to make the divine picture complete. There are no free-lancers in God's economy ! We all need the spiritual ministries of one another if we are to fulfill God's full will.

The new power which God desires to progressively release through the lives of Spirit-filled believers should be channeled back into one's local church ! It is suggested that unless God leads otherwise one should share their Pentecostal experience in the Holy Spirit with their pastor. Carefully explain how real Jesus Christ has become to your life and your deep desire to glorify Him in ways of Christian love. Assure your pastor, if he seems unduly concerned, that anytime he might feel it would be desirable, you will be happy to quietly withdraw in Christian love; but until then you feel your place is in the fellowship of the church. This will place a responsibility upon you to live a Christ-honoring, Spirit-filled life. It will also place the responsibility for any possible separation in fellowship upon others.

Real truth needs no defense; it will authenticate itself ! One need never feel they have to defend themselves or God. All we are required to do is manifest Jesus Christ through our lives by His Spirit. We can always be ready to share the Gifts of God's Son and His Spirit with others as He provides the opportunity, but never is there any occasion for argument. This does not mean that there will not be opposition. The real test of brokeness before the Lord may come during times of unfair criticism and even persecution. Purpose in your heart to follow your Lord whatever the cost. There is no sweeter reward in all of life than to know you are in the center of His will, and God's will is Jesus, simply Jesus.

It is also imperative to find fellowship with other Spirit-filled believers if you are going to grow in the full purpose for which He has called you by His Spirit. There is the need to be further grounded in the Word as it is broken in Christian fellowship. You will also find that there are others who are going, or have gone, through the same valleys of possible doubts and discouragement which you may be facing. Furthermore, oftentimes our needs whether physical or spiritual may be met through the ministry of all the spiritual gifts (1 Corinthians 12:8-10). The very purpose of God's good gifts is to edify the Body and glorify the Head who is Jesus. You are an important part of the Body and in living union with the Head.

Also, as we grow in our spiritual life, we shall find God sovereignly prompting us to move out by faith into the exercise of some of the spiritual gifts. As your own ministry develops, you may find in God's grace that you are "excelling" more in some gifts than in others to the benefit of fellow believers. To learn and to grow with others is a mutually profitable experience.

Without Christian fellowship with Spirit-filled believers, all too often the faithless influence of others concerning the significance of His spiritual gifts will darken our sense of bright expectation. Once our faith is so dampened, the streams of God's Spirit in new and powerful ways will slacken, and we will find ourselves back in a "life as usual" sort of an existence. *Those who "move in" and "move on" nearly always are those who have continued to sharpen their newfound spiritual experience in warm Christian fellowship.* We just have not been created to "go it alone"! A sustained lack of fellowship will almost always quench even the brightest flame of God's Spirit in a life. We need one another! God has admonished us in His Word to forsake not the assembling of ourselves together but to exhort and encourage one another all the more as we see the day approaching (Hebrews 10:25).

Follow that prompting of God's Spirit for spiritual fellowship! Actually, Christian fellowship is the natural outcome and desire of an overflowing life in the Spirit. *Go with an expectation of both sharing and receiving.* Paul's pattern for a Spirit-filled meeting is that each participant should have a hymn, or a teaching, or a revelation, or an utterance in an unknown tongue or an interpretation of it. But let everything be constructive and edifying and for the good of all (1 Corinthians 14:26, Amplified New Testament).

We have experienced many times of fellowship in home prayer-and-share meetings that have followed this scriptural pattern. We have seen God's Spirit through His servants and by His gifts manifest God's Son in marvelous ways. There have been times of soul-searching and correction. There have been occasions of tenderness of God's Spirit sweetly moved across the hearts of sensitive believers. At other times the whole group has joined in beautiful songs in the Spirit where both words and music were of a heavenly nature. Here is true worship in the beauty of holiness. Sometimes God would move powerfully and in spectacular ways to bring physical deliverance and healing. Perhaps after the ministry of God's Word, the Holy Spirit would bring meaningful confirmation to hearts and minds through prophecy or tongues and interpretation.

Often those who lack faith to receive the Holy Spirit

in His fullness by themselves will find in the faith and wisdom of other Spirit-filled believers all the added encouragement that is needed. *Fellowship builds faith !*

The ways of God's choosing for meeting the needs of His people are unpredictable for any given meeting. His purpose, however, is always the same: To encourage, strengthen and quicken the believers, and magnify His Son — *to edify the Body and glorify the Head.* This is the fundamental principle for Christian fellowship of any kind. Every participant should be governed by this rule. The Holy Spirit will *always* honor with His manifest Presence *every* meeting that is so centered in God's Son. This is God's pattern for His people.

Real fellowship will follow through in real life. The consequence of sharing Jesus with fellow believers is a desire to also share Him with unbelievers. "That which we have seen and heard declare we unto you, *that ye also may have fellowship with us,"* and truly our fellowship is with the Father, and with His Son Jesus Christ" (1 John 1:3,4). The Body of Christ possess *Life.* "Life begets Life"! Once we have experienced real *Life* there is an overwhelming desire to share it with others. Basically that is what real spiritual fellowship is: the sharing of this *Life.* Jesus said, "I am . . . *the* life." Fellowship is simply sharing Jesus !

To be filled with the Spirit is to be filled with a desire to share Jesus with one another !

CHAPTER XIII

The Spirit of Peace

The fast, feverish, high-pressured pace of our modern world has produced an atmosphere which is not conducive to inner peace of heart. Far too often our lives are characterized by an inner agitation or restlessness of soul. Stress, strain, fear, and worry make their marks, and man's soul cries out for relief. It is even possible for the spirit of this age to spill over into our Christian life, and we can become so frantic in our service for the Lord that we succeed more in wearing ourselves out than in gaining solid ground for God in our lives or in the lives of others.

For the Spirit-filled Christian, however, there is the promise of inner peace and rest. There is a serenity of mind and repose for the soul which enables us to maintain a spiritual poise regardless of circumstances. Real life demands more than pretty promises and sweet sentiment. There must be a solid center to our lives which remains unmoved and untouched by the storms of life and the turmoil of our times. *That center is Christ !*

Let us explore this in a more specific way. Peace and rest are far more than just abstract characteristics of the Christian life. These words are more than just wishful thoughts or expressions of soft sentiment. Each one is a reference to something which is as solid as concrete and as strong as tempered steel. That something is really Someone. *That Someone is Jesus Christ !* Jesus Christ is what makes our Christianity concrete. When the Holy

Spirit fills us with the Life of our Lord, He is putting
steel into our soul. Peace is a person; rest is a person. *That
Person is Jesus Christ !* He is the solid center of our lives.

Now we can only stay "on center" when we by faith
allow the Holy Spirit to have full and complete control of
our lives. If we are restless or lose our inner harmony of
heart, we have moved "off center" in some area of our
experience. All we have to do is ask the Holy Spirit to
recentralize our lives. This He will do by many ways and
means. Usually, He will simply begin *with us,* and suggest
that we acquaint now *ourselves* with Him and be at
peace (Job 22:21). It is impossible to get better acquainted
with Jesus and not be at peace because *He is peace.* It is
the desire of the blessed Comforter to help us get better
acquainted with Jesus just at such times as we need Him
most.

The pathway of God's will is the pathway of peace.
Here is a very positive principle that should give direction
to every Spirit-filled believer. If any situation destroys
your inner harmony of heart, quiet yourself before Him.
Ask the Holy Spirit of truth to reveal to you if something
is off center. It may be your doubts (misplaced faith). Ask
God to square your faith with Scripture. Center your trust
in His Word. To trust His Word when feelings and even
reason may indicate otherwise will bring His peace.

On the other hand, your uneasiness may be a sense of
discernment that Jesus is not finding the place He desires
to have. Any situation which does not direct our full at-
tention to the Lord is partially off center. A truly Christ-
centered life will quickly detect this. It may begin merely
as a feeling of uneasiness, but as we seek God's Spirit to
relate things to Jesus, He will bring discernment of a more
specific nature !

The principle of peace finds very practical application

when we face the many decisions which confront us in everyday life. *Every day is a day of decision !* Sometimes they are little decisions and sometimes big decisions that can change our entire lives. If we learn how to make the little decisions, we will know how to face the big ones. The way in which we face the decisions of today may well determine those of tomorrow.

For the Spirit-filled Christian this way is the way of peace. Without inner peace of heart it is impossible to sense God's will or hear His voice. Sometimes His voice is very still and very small. Purposefully so ! The inner noise of confusion and unrest will completely drown it out. The remedy for such inner distress is simply the presence of Christ. One touch of His hand can calm the troubled waters of our soul.

How easy it is for us to stray from the Way of Peace. But when we do we hear a word behind us saying "this is the way walk ye in it" (Isaiah 30:21). Jesus tenderly reminds us that *He is that way* (John 14:6). Upon returning *to Him* we find inner rest, and in such quietness and confidence we find inner strength (Isaiah 30:15). *It is as we rest in Him that we can go forth in His name !* (2 Chronicles 14:11). Let us therefore acquaint ourselves with Him and be at peace (Job 22:21). And, "Let the peace (soul harmony which comes) from the Christ rule in your hearts — deciding and settling with finality all questions that arise in your minds — (in that peaceful state) . . . be thankful — appreciative, giving praise to God always" (Colossians 3:15, Amplified New Testament).

To be filled with the Spirit is to be filled with Peace !

CHAPTER XIV

The Spirit of Holiness

The Greek root word for holiness is "hagios." From the same root come the related English words, sanctification and saint. The corresponding root word in Hebrew is "gadash." The range of meaning in English is found in the verbs: *dedicate, consecrate, sanctify, hallow, venerate, cleanse, purify* and *perfect.*

To many people holiness and sanctification are practically synonomous with a narrow, gloomy, joyless type of existence. They tend to equate a holy life with a hollow life. Nothing could be further from the truth, and how Satan would desire to perpetuate this lie. To see clearly the blind and blurred areas in our understanding of true holiness, we must first look to Jesus and see the whole matter as related to Him. *The heavenly pattern of holiness for the earthly saint is found in God's Son.* He alone is *the* Holy One. Let us see what this means to us personally.

The Apostle Peter relates the holy life to our "call" and to our "conduct." "Like obedient children, do not shape your lives by the cravings which were formerly yours in the time of your ignorance, but, in imitation of the Holy One who has called you, do you also be holy in all your behavior; since it is written, 'you are to be holy, because I am holy'" (1 Peter 1:14-16, Weymouth).

The word "saint" means a *called-out-one.* The primary requisite for sainthood is to hear the call of Christ and respond to His claims upon our lives. "My sheep *hear* my

voice . . . and they *follow* me" (John 10:27). This is the
simple two-fold basis for the life of holiness. *To hear and
to follow speaks of our calling and our conduct.*

The door and the way to the saintly life is both straight
and narrow. "Strait is the gate, and narrow is the way,
which leadeth unto life" (Matthew 7:14). Note this pas-
sage is not referring so much to *a way of life* as it is to
the way to life. Jesus simultaneously is the door, the way,
and the life. He said so ! "I am the Door. Anyone, who
enters in through Me will be saved — will live," (John
10:9, Amplified New Testament). "I am the Way and
the Truth and the Life; no one comes to the Father except
my Me" (John 14:6). There is only *one* true door, *one*
true way, and *one* true life ! The Bible rather directly nar-
rows the range of possibilities by which we can find the
true life of holiness to one. That one possibility is a per-
son, and that person is Jesus Christ. The life of holiness
is the life that Christ *is*. "Be ye holy for I am holy." *Sancti-
fication is the process by which the Holy Spirit conforms
us into the holy image of God's Son.*

The twofold pattern of calling and conduct is beauti-
fully illustrated for us in the life of Christ. Jesus was a
marked man from his birth. He was called to be the Sav-
iour of the world. Even the name Jesus Christ in the orig-
inal languages refers to His Saviourhood and Messiahship.
He was called to be a man of destiny. His life was lived
with a divine sense of mission and purpose. Every minute
of His life was meaningful. Every encounter He had with
people was divinely ordered. Every circumstance of His
life was charged with eternal significance. Everything
pointed in one divine direction. His only desire and great
delight was to fulfill the will of His Father. He set His
face like a flint and allowed nothing to swerve Him from
fufilling His divine destiny. The conduct of His life re-

flected the commitment of His soul. There was a discipline to each day which was related to the direction of His life. His motives were pure. His life was clean. His heart was perfect. He was moved with compassion but was never mastered by feeling. Communication with the Father was constantly clear. His life was perfectly transparent and never once was it clouded with the sin of selfishness. The eternal purposes of heaven were ever so real that the temporal pleasures of the world never possessed His life. He was in the world but not of the world. He hated sin but loved the sinner. He sat with the sinners but was never soiled by their sin. To touch His life at any time or in any place or with any one was to touch the holiness of God. Indeed He was the sinless Son of God. *Jesus Christ was absolutely and altogether holy!*

With great feeling we now respond to our Lord's clear call to us, "Be ye holy, for I am holy." We are both amazed and humbled at such a high and holy calling. *As sons of God we too have become marked men and women from the day of our spiritual birth.* And as fantastic as it seems our Lord emphatically declares that as the Father sent Him, so sends He us to live a holy life in a most unholy world. The implications of our calling can be as frustrating and discouraging as they are amazing until we realize it is going to be accomplished in His way not ours.

Once again we are directed to the third Person of the Trinity. He is God's way to personal holiness. As His name implies, He is the very Spirit of holiness. *It is His ministry to progressively reveal and release the holiness of Christ in and through our lives.* I remember an Episcopalian friend of ours who rather vividly expressed it this way, "After I was filled with the Holy Spirit, I soon discovered that He was just waiting to take His little broom and begin housecleaning."

As the light of God's Spirit shines fully into our lives, a lifetime accumulation of trash, dust and cobwebs comes to our attention and His. He requests permission to clean up one area of our life after another. If given free reign, we discover He works with amazing swiftness and most efficiently. His housecleaning tools are varied and some are most unusual. In fact, at the time we may never even recognize them as such. It is only after all is said and done that we realize another room has become clean and bright.

We never readily appreciate how many rooms, closets and cupboards there are in these earthly temples of ours until God begins His work of cleansing. Some areas are so easily and quickly brightened up that we aren't even aware of the change until some time later. Then to our surprise we notice that some musty corner of our life that had been a little dark and dingy before is now fresh and clean. Other areas seem to require rather persistent scrubbing and to our dismay are so easily soiled again. However, by quickly submitting to the purifying power of God's forgiving Spirit as soon as the stains of sin are discovered, even these parts of our lives will become shining examples of God's perfecting power.

Occasionally the Holy Spirit will come to a closet in these lives of ours which remains closed to His presence. Knowing that Jesus could never be completely at home in a life where forbidden areas remained, He kindly but insistently asks us for the key. To resist His persistent plea brings conflict and confusion into our lives. We quickly realize that we are facing a far greater issue than the particular one with which the Holy Spirit confronts us. The real issue centers in the professed Lordship of Jesus Christ. If we are not completely mastered by Jesus Christ, then He is not really Master at all, for us ! *The Holy Spirit's deep*

*desire for you and me is that Christ Jesus be Lord of all
. . . all of you and all of me !*

True holiness can never be cataloged as a list of do's
and don'ts. *Rather it is an attitude of heart that lovingly
recognizes the Lordship of Jesus Christ.* We become will-
ing bondslaves of our loving Lord. We are as committed
to Him through the bonds of love as He was committed
to the will o fthe Father.

Real holiness is a love relationship. A wedding ring is
a seal and a symbol of eternal and undivided love. It is a
love gift from the groom to the bride. The Spirit of Holi-
ness is Christ's love gift to His Bride. It is the seal of our
holy union with Him in salvation. It was a costly gift, and
Jesus paid the full price. He gave Himself, all of Him-
self, that we through the Holy Spirit might intimately and
personally know the life and love of God. Jesus was utter-
ly and completely broken that we might have unbroken
communion with Him.

It all becomes so clear in the light of God's love. *Holi-
ness is Calvary !* An all out surrender to the love and will
of God, that His love and will might find full expression
in our lives. How trite and trivial becomes the life that
tries to calculate how far he can go without being labeled
"worldly".

So often we have a tendency to logically construct an
artificial list of worldly do's and don'ts as if holiness of
heart could be measured by men's minds. God's standard
of holiness so far transcends any yardstick that we might
project that we would do better to look first to His Son
and then to the world. It is possible to become so possessed
by the negative attitude of avoiding the world that we al-
most become more worldly-minded than the sinner who
unconsciously is a part of it. How much better to be so
possessed by the love of Jesus Christ that we always aim

to order our behavior in such a way as to continually promote His presence in our lives and the lives of others. *He then becomes our standard of holiness. The more His measure increases in our lives the more wholesomely holy do we naturally become.*

To be wedded to God's Son speaks of a life of holy adventure. We have dedicated ourselves to the exciting purpose of knowing Him and sharing Him with others. We jealously guard against anything that would so possess our body, mind or spirit that our daily communion with Him or witness for Him might become clouded or confused. This is a most exacting but divinely exhilarating way to live. This is life as it was meant to be!

A truly holy life is also a very lovely life. It is a life in which nothing detracts from the beauty of the indwelling Christ. Just as we would never display a magnificent work of art in a cheap, gaudy picture frame, so our lives must suitably frame the lovely portrait of our Lord. The sensitive Christian will be very careful concerning extremes in conversation, conduct or dress. Our desire is to allow our lives to become an attractive setting for His presence.

The principles which we have just shared together have very practical, present-tense applications. As we yield our total being to the Holy Spirit, He will faithfully and progressively deal with various dimensions of our lives which need His sanctifying touch. To realize that God desires to freshen and cleanse new areas of our lives each day lends a holy excitement to our Christian experience. He doesn't always begin at the same place in each life, and we must be careful not to gauge the spiritual progress of others by the precise way in which He is working in ours. God begins where we are and with the areas of greatest need. Let us allow Him to do His work in His way in our lives and in the lives of others. If we continue to encourage one another in the Spirit, He will faithfully proceed with His perfecting work.

What we think, say, and do; where we go; what we listen to and look at; how we budget our time and order our our lives; even how we care for our physical bodies will all come under the silent scrutiny of God's Holy Spirit. With expectations we will listen to hear what suggestions He will make and how He will enable us to meet the challenge of the disciplined life.

We will soon discover that there may be some things that others can do that we cannot. We will be careful, however, not to judge others remembering the converse is also true. Also, many things that now seem to be such a permanent part of our life may strangely lose their importance as better things take their place. God will continually be leading us from the harmful to the good, to the better, to the best. At each step we find new freedom and wonder why we previously were so attached to nonessentials.

The theme of personal holiness takes on a timely significance when we see it related to the character of the Church just prior to our Lord's return. Paul shares with us the desires of the Heavenly Bridegroom that His Bride, the Church, should be sanctified, cleansed and washed. In fact, she is to be presented as a glorious Church without blemish (Ephesians 5:26,27).

The end-time Church is also going to be characterized as a militant church. She will be consecrated for the purpose of a great worldwide witness unto all the nations. ". . . then shall the end come" (Matthew 24:14). This twofold character of *purity* and *power* will be the result of the *sanctifying* and *unifying* work of the Holy Spirit who in these last days is being poured out upon all flesh.

As individual members of the Church, we should relate our lives to the lateness of the hour in a meaningful

way. The secular world is certainly aware of the unique-
ness of our atomic age. *The Bulletin of the Atomic Sci-
entists* is a publication which is dedicated to the peculiar
problems of our times. On the cover of every issue is the
face of a clock, the hands of which are set at five minutes
to twelve. No one knows when the clock may strike, but
there is an awareness that time may be shorter than we
think. The newspaper headlines daily reinforce this feel-
ing of uneasiness.

As Christians we are told that when the signs of the
end-time begin to appear, we are to look up for our re-
demption draweth nigh. In other words, we are to lift our
heads and be alert and allow the second coming of Christ
to be a *purifying hope* which quickens our desire to re-
deem the time and live life with eternity in full view.
Perhaps we need to feel the same sense of commitment to
God's holy will as did Jesus when He realized His hour
was fast approaching. *Our hour may be closer upon us
than we realize!*

What a motivating and purifying hope the soon return
of the Lord becomes to our daily lives. The Holy Scriptures
would even indicate that we can hasten the day of His
appearance by keeping our lives filled with His Spirit of
purity and power. As we encourage others to be continual-
ly filled with God's Spirit, we are actually playing a neces-
sary part in preparing the Bride of Christ for her Bride-
groom ! Surely in view of our times we can make Peter's
admonition our daily prayer. "What manner of persons
ought (we) to be in all holy conversation and godliness,
looking for and hastening unto the coming of the day of
God . . ." (2 Peter 3:11, 12).

Recently my wife and I prayed that God would confirm
the sense of urgency in our lives which we have associated
with the soon return of our Lord. I felt almost compelled

to request that God would answer our prayer within the week if it were His will. The next morning I received a letter in the mail from an attorney in Los Angeles who has recently been filled with God's Spirit. The Lord had awakened him at 12:25 A.M. a few days previously, and the Holy Spirit had given him the following prophecy:

"Now we must all work together in the Spirit. Call on each dear brother as the need arises. Tell your problems freely. Ask for counsel and guidance. When a dear brother calls you, respond without question. There is much to be done throughout the world. There must be a harmonious blending of the talents of all those blessed with the Holy Spirit. Each will have a special gift to contribute to this great undertaking in God's work in these latter days. The time is short I say again and again and again. These are not idle words. People must be made to realize this. You are to make this urgency known through those with the Holy Spirit. Then the message will fan out and reach all peoples everywhere. All must be given their chance to accept Jesus and the Cross before it is too late. *Stress the lateness of the hour in everything you do for the Lord and in all your testimony, preaching and witnessing.* Those not saved must be reached by every method and means and channel available to man. They must be told of the shortness of time in which to make their decision for Jesus Christ, Saviour and Redeemer. Talk of this message whenever you are able. Our Heavenly Father is grieved because many alive today will not be saved because they foolishly think there is ample time remaining for salvation. In this, I repeat, they are wrong. Time is very short. The day of reckoning is near. The fulfillment of the Divine Plan is nigh at hand. Let all take heed and turn toward the Cross. Man's blindness to this message will be his undoing. His eyes must be opened, and the light of our dear Lord

Jesus must shine through to his soul and consciousness. The Holy Spirit will lead and guide in this movement of the Lord. Give Him free reign and surrender and be obedient to His instructions. This is a clear call for action by all Spirit-filled people everywhere to move in God's work."

Here, we see again our high and holy calling. May we daily consecrate and dedicate our lives to God's holy will without reservation. May we expectantly listen to His voice of instruction and then obediently follow our heavenly and holy Shepherd in the path of purity and power. "Even so, come Lord Jesus."

To be filled with the Holy Spirit is to be filled with purifying hope.

CHAPTER XV

The Spirit of Love

What better topic could we choose with which to conclude our time in sharing together than that of love. God is love! We see His love expressed for us in Jesus. Calvary love is much more than sweet sentiment. It is the very heartbeat of God. *Love not only is; it gives!* The Father gave us His heart when He gave us His Son. He exhausted the very treasury of heaven that we might have fellowship with Him. In ourselves we are not worthy of His love, but He loves us anyway!

The love of John 3:16 is expressed by the Greek word "agape." It is the highest and noblest word for love. In the New Testament it takes on a divine dimension that gives it an infinite value. It is the kind of love that is characterized by the subject loving—God. It is further characterized by the value and preciousness of the object loved— you and me. God considers us to be of infinite value because of the divine purpose for which we were created— that we might be conformed into His image ! *Agape love is Calvary love.*

The Holy Spirit is the Spirit of love. His overwhelming desire is to fill us with the love that God is. "For God's love has been poured out in our hearts through the Holy Spirit Who has been given to us" (Romans 5:5, Amplified New Testatment).

The fruit and the gifts of the Spirit are expressions of God's love. The fruit of the Spirit as found in Galatians

5:22 and 23 is but a variation of love in its *being* or *character*. Love, joy, gladness, peace, are what love is *within;* longsuffering, patience, gentleness, goodness are what love is *toward man;* faithfulness, meekness (humility), temperance (self-control) are what love is *toward God.*

The gifts of the Spirit as found in 1 Corinthians 12:8-10 are expressions of God's love in *thought, word* and *deed.* Wisdom, knowledge, discernment are love in *thought;* prophecy, tongues, interpretations are love in *word;* faith, healings, miracles are love in *deed.*

Without the full complement of the fruit and gifts of the Spirit, God's love is incomplete to and through His Church. With the present outpouring of the Holy Spirit, we are seeing the Spirit of love completing His ministry in the Church. This is how the Church is to become as fresh and full of promise as the morning; as fair as the still, cool beauty of the moon; as bright as the warm revealing sun and as terrible as an aggressive victorious army with banners. (Songs of Solomon 6:10). *Love is fresh, fair, bright, and powerful!* Does not Calvary speak of promise, rest, light, and victory? This is the gospel of the Cross. This is our message to a hopeless, restless, darkened, sin-shackled world. Through His love God has provided deliverance for body, soul and spirit. Can we do any less than shout to a dying world, "Look to His love and live!"

Everywhere there are hearts literally longing for God's Love ! I remember two very vivid experiences related to this. One concerned a young seminary student who was interested in the baptism with the Holy Spirit for his life. We had talked with him for a while and were about to pray together when he broke down and pleaded with us to pray that God would somehow reveal to him His love. I can still feel and hear the desperate cry of his heart as he longed to know that God loved him *personally.* The

Holy Spirit prompted us with a word of wisdom which we immediately shared with him. "How could God any more clearly and forcefully show His great love for you personally than He did when He gave His own Son?"

Calvary love is terribly real, and he responded immediately to this real assurance that God graciously provided. How long he had carried this burden I do not know, but I somehow feel that there may be those next to us whom we least suspect that are likewise longing for an assurance that God loves them.

On another occasion we were counseling with the wife of a pastor who too was interested in the fullness of God's Spirit for her life. In the course of our prayer together the Lord brought through us a brief prophecy concerning His interest, concern and love for her. "Oh," she cried, "does God *really* love me? For a whole year I have been going through a valley of darkness and have wondered many times if God still loved me." This assurance of God's love to which the Holy Spirit witnessed brought peace and joy to her heart.

There is no greater privilege than to share the love of Jesus with others! May His Spirit so fill our lives with the love of God that anytime, anyplace, anywhere, others may be able to look to us and know that God loves them.

We now share with you this last thought, and really it is the most important of all for *everything else* rests upon it. *To be filled with the Holy Spirit is to be filled with Calvary love!* "For God so loved . . . that he gave" Can we do less?

Appendix

*"And ye shall seek me, and find me,
when ye shall search for me with all
your heart." (Jeremiah 29:13)*

*"They received the word with all
readiness of mind, and searched the
scriptures daily, whether those things
were so." (Acts 17:11)*

I Personal Promises for Holy Spirit Baptism

1. And it shall come to pass afterward, that I will pour out my spirit upon all flesh; and your sons and your daughters shall prophesy, your old men shall dream dreams, your young men shall see visions: And also upon the servants and upon the handmaids in those days will I pour out my spirit. (Joel 2:28,29)

2. In those days came John the Baptist, preaching in the wilderness of Judaea, and saying, Repent ye: for the kingdom of heaven is at hand. I indeed baptize you with water unto repentance: but he (Jesus) that cometh after me is mightier than I, whose shoes I am not worthy to bear: he shall baptize you with the Holy Ghost, and with fire: (Matt. 3:1,2,11)

3. He that believeth on me (Jesus), as the scripture hath said, out of his belly shall flow rivers of living water. But this spake he of the Spirit, which they that believe on him should receive: for the Holy Ghost was not yet given; because that Jesus was not yet glorified. (John 7:38,39)

4. And I (Jesus) will pray the Father, and he shall give you another Comforter, that he may abide with you for ever; even the Spirit of truth; whom the world cannot receive, because it seeth him not, neither knoweth him: but ye know

i

him; for he dwelleth with you, and shall be in you. But the Comforter, which is the Holy Ghost, whom the Father will send in my name, he shall teach you all things, and bring all things to your remembrance, whatsoever I have said unto you. (John 14:16,17,26)

5. But when the Comforter is come, whom I (Jesus) will send unto you from the Father, even the Spirit of truth, which proceedeth from the Father, he shall testify of me: (John 15:26)

6. Nevertheless I (Jesus) tell you the truth; It is expedient for you that I go away: for if I go not away, the Comforter will not come unto you; but if I depart, I will send him unto you. I have yet many things to say unto you, but ye cannot bear them now. Howbeit when he, the Spirit of truth, is come, he will guide you into all truth: for he shall not speak of himself; but whatsoever he shall hear, that shall he speak: and he will shew you things to come. He shall glorify me: for he shall receive of mine, and shall shew it unto you. (John 16:7,12,13,14)

7. And, being assembled together with them, (Jesus) commanded them (the disciples) that they should not depart from Jerusalem, but wait for the promise of the Father, which, saith he, ye have heard of me. For John truly baptized with water; but ye shall be baptized with the Holy Ghost not many days hence. But ye shall receive power, after that the Holy Ghost is come upon you: and ye shall be witnesses unto me both in Jerusalem, and in all Judaea, and in Samaria, and unto the uttermost part of the earth. (Acts 1:4,5,8)

II The Promises Personally Fulfilled

1. And when the day of Pentecost was fully come, they (disciples) were all with one accord in one place. And suddenly there came a sound from heaven as of a rushing mighty wind, and it filled all the house where they were sitting. And there appeared unto them cloven tongues like as of fire, and it sat upon each of them. And they were all filled with the Holy Ghost, and began to speak with other tongues, as the Spirit gave them utterance. Now when this was noised

abroad, the multitude came together, and were confounded, because that every man heard them speak in his own language. And they were all amazed and marvelled, saying one to another, Behold, are not all these which speak Galilaens? We do hear them speak in our tongues the wonderful works of God. And they were all amazed, and were in doubt, saying one to another, What meaneth this? Others mocking said, These men are full of new wine. (Acts 2:1-4,6,7,11-13)

2. But Peter, standing up with the eleven, lifted up his voice, and said unto them, Ye men of Judea, and all ye that dwell at Jerusalem, be this known unto you, and hearken to my words: For these are not drunken, as ye suppose, seeing it is but the third hour of the day. But this is that which was spoken by the prophet Joel; And it shall come to pass in the last days, saith God, I will pour out my Spirit upon all flesh: and your sons and your daughters shall prophesy, and your young men shall see visions, and your old men shall dream dreams: And on my servants and on my handmaidens I will pour out in those days of my Spirit; and they shall prophesy: (Acts 2:14-18)

3. Ye men of Israel, hear these words; Jesus of Nazareth, a man approved of God among you by miracles and wonders and signs, which God did by him in the midst of you, as ye yourselves also know: Him, being delivered by the determinate counsel and foreknowledge of God, ye have taken, and by wicked hands have crucified and slain: This Jesus hath God raised up, whereof we all are witnesses. Therefore being by the right hand of God exalted, and having received of the Father the promise of the Holy Ghost, he hath shed forth this, which ye now see and hear. (Acts: 2:22,23,32,33)

III The Pattern For Personal Fulfillment

1. Now when they heard this, they were pricked in their heart, and said unto Peter and to the rest of the apostles, Men and brethren, what shall we do? Then Peter said unto them, Repent ,and be baptized every one of you in the name of Jesus Christ for the remission of sins, and ye shall receive the gift of the Holy Ghost. For the promise is unto you, and to your children, and to all that are afar off, even as many

as the Lord our God shall call. Then they that gladly received his word were baptized: and the same day there were added unto them about three thousands souls. (Acts 2:37-39,41)

2. Then Philip went down to the city of Samaria, and preached Christ unto them. But when they believed Philip preaching the things concerning the kingdom of God, and the name of Jesus Christ, they were baptized, both men and women. Now when the apostles which were at Jerusalem heard that Samaria had received the word of God, they sent unto them Peter and John: Who, when they were come down, prayed for them, that they might receive the Holy Ghost: For as yet he was fallen upon none of them: only they were baptized in the name of the Lord Jesus. Then laid they their hands on them, and they received the Holy Ghost. (Acts 8:5,12,14-17)

3. And Ananias went his way, and entered into the house; and putting his hands on him said, Brother Saul, the Lord, even Jesus, that appeared unto thee in the way thou camest, hath sent me, that thou mightest receive thy sight, and be filled with the Holy Ghost. And immediately there fell from his eyes as it had been scales: and he received sight forthwith, and arose, and was baptized. (Acts 9:17,18)

4. And as Peter was coming in, Cornelius (a devout gentile centurion) met him, and fell down at his feet, and worshipped him. But Peter took him up, saying, Stand up; I myself also am a man. And as he talked with him, he went in, and found many that were come together. And he said unto them, Ye know how that it is an unlawful thing for a man that is a Jew to keep company, or come unto one of another nation; but God hath shewed me that I should not call any man common or unclean.
Then Peter opened his mouth, and said, Of a truth I perceive that God is no respecter of persons: But in every nation he that feareth him, and worketh righteousness, is accepted with him. The word which God sent unto the children of Israel, preaching peace by Jesus Christ: he is Lord of all: That word, I say, ye know, which was published throughout all Judaea, and began from Galilee, after the baptism which John preached; How God anointed Jesus

of Nazareth with the Holy Ghost and with power: who went about doing good, and healing all that were oppressed of the devil; for God was with him. And we are witnesses of all things which he did both in the land of the Jews, and in Jerusalem; whom they slew and hanged on a tree: Him God raised up the third day, and shewed him openly; Not to all people, but unto witnesses chosen before of God, even to us, who did eat and drink with him after he rose from the dead. And he commanded us to preach unto the people, and to testify that it is he which was ordained of God to be the Judge of quick and dead. To him give all the prophets witness, and through his name whosoever believeth in him shall receive remission of sins.

While Peter yet spake these words, the Holy Ghost fell on them which heard the word. And they of the circumcision (Jews) which believed were astonished, as many as came with Peter, because that on the Gentiles also was poured out the gift of the Holy Ghost. For they heard them speak with tongues, and magnify God. Then answered Peter, Can any man forbid water, that these should not be baptized, which have received the Holy Ghost as well as we? And he commanded them to be baptized in the name of the Lord. Then prayed they him to tarry certain days. (Acts 10:25-28,34-48)

5. And the apostles and (Jewish) brethren that were in Judaea heard that the Gentiles had also received the word of God. And when Peter was come up to Jerusalem they that were of the circumcision contended with him, Saying Thou wentest in to men uncircumcised, and didst eat with them. But Peter rehearsed the matter from the beginning, and expounded it by order unto them, saying, . . . And as I began to speak (to the Gentiles), the Holy Ghost fell on them, as on us at the beginning. Then remembered I the word of the Lord, how that he said, John indeed baptized with water; but ye shall be baptized with the Holy Ghost. Forasmuch then as God gave them the like gift as he did unto us, who believed on the Lord Jesus Christ; what was I, that I could withstand God? When they heard these things, they held their peace, and glorified God. (Acts 11:1-4,15-18a)

6. And it came to pass, that while Apollos was at Corinth,

Paul having passed through the upper coasts came to Ephesus: and finding certain disciples, He said unto them, Have ye received the Holy Ghost since ye believed? And they said unto him, We have not so much as heard whether there be any Holy Ghost. And he said unto them, Unto what then were ye baptized? And they said, Unto John's baptism. Then said Paul, John verily baptized with the baptism of repentance, saying unto the people, that they should believe on him which should come after him, that is, on Christ Jesus. When they heard this, they were baptized in the name of the Lord Jesus. And when Paul had laid his hands upon them, the Holy Ghost came on them; and they spake with tongues, and prophesied. And all the men were about twelve. (Acts 19:1-7)

IV Personally Appropriated By Faith

1. This only would I (Paul) learn of you, Received ye the Spirit by the works of the law, or by the hearing of faith? That the blessing of Abraham might come on the Gentiles through Jesus Christ; that we might receive the promise of the Spirit through faith. (Gal. 3:2,14)

2. He that believeth on me (Jesus), as the scripture hath said, out of his belly shall flow rivers of living water. But this spake he of the Spirit, which they that believe on him should receive: for the Holy Ghost was not yet given; because that Jesus was not yet glorified. (John 7:38,39)

3. And I (Jesus) say unto you, Ask, and it shall be given you; seek, and ye shall find; knock, and it shall be opened unto you. For everyone that asketh receiveth; and he that seeketh findeth; and to him that knocketh it shall be opened. If a son shall ask bread of any of you that is a father, will he give him a stone? or if he ask a fish, will he for a fish give him a serpent? Or if he shall ask an egg, will he offer him a scorpion? If ye then, being evil, know how to give good gifts unto your children: how much more shall your heavenly Father give the Holy Spirit to them that ask him? (Luke 11:9-13)

V The Privilege of Inspired Prayer and Praise for Personal Devotions

1. After my words they spake not again; and my speech dropped upon them. And they waited for me as for the rain; and they opened their mouths wide as for the latter rain. (Job 29:22,23)

2. Open thy mouth wide, and I will fill it. (Psa. 81:10b)

3. For with stammering lips and another tongue will he speak to this people. To whom he said, This is the rest wherewith ye may cause the weary to rest; and this is the refreshing: yet they would not hear. (Isa. 28:11,12)

4. And they were all filled with the Holy Ghost, and began to speak with other tongues, as the Spirit gave them utterance. (Acts 2:4)

5. While Peter yet spake these words, the Holy Ghost fell upon them which heard the word. For they heard them speak with tongues, and magnify God. (Acts 10:44,46)

6. And when Paul had laid his hands upon them, the Holy Ghost came on them; and they spake with tongues, and prophesied. (Acts 19:6)

7. And these signs shall follow them that believe; In my name they shall cast out devils; they shall speak with new tongues. (Mark 16:17)

8. I (Paul) thank my God I speak in tongues more than ye all (in private devotions) . . . (For) he that speaketh in an unknown tongue edifieth himself . . . (and) verily givest thanks well. He that speaketh in an unknown tongue, speaketh not unto men, but unto God: for no man understandeth him; howbeit in the spirit he speaketh mysteries. For if I pray in an unknown tongue, my spirit prayeth, but my understanding is unfruitful. (I Cor. 14:18,4,17,2,14)

9. The Spirit also helpeth our infirmities: for we know not what we should pray for as we ought: but the Spirit itself maketh intercession for us with groanings which cannot be uttered. And he that searcheth the hearts knoweth what is the mind of the Spirit, because he maketh intercession for the saints according to the will of God. (Rom. 8:26,27)

10. But ye, beloved, building up yourselves on your most holy faith, praying in the Holy Ghost. (Jude 20)

11. Praying always with all prayer and supplication in the Spirit,

and watching thereunto with all perseverance and supplication for all saints. (Eph. 6:18)

12. By him therefore let us offer the sacrifice of praise to God continually, that is, the fruit of our lips giving thanks to his name. (Heb. 13:15)

13. Let my prayer be set forth before thee as incense: and the lifting up of my hands as the evening sacrifice. (Psa. 141:2)

14. For they heard them speak with tongues, and magnify God. (Acts 10:46

15. O magnify the Lord with me, and let us exalt his name together. (Psa. 34:3)

16. I will bless the Lord at all times: his praise shall continually be in my mouth. (Psa. 34:1)

VI Marks of the Spirit-filled Christian

1. And they were all *filled* with the Holy Ghost, and began to speak with other tongues, as the Spirit gave them utterance. (Acts 2:4)

2. And now, Lord, behold their threatenings: and grant unto thy servants, that with all boldness they may speak thy word, by stretching forth thine hand to heal; and that signs and wonders may be done by the name of thy holy child Jesus. And when they had prayed, the place was shaken where they were assembled together; and they were *filled* with the Holy Ghost, and they spake the word of God with boldness. (Acts 4:29-31)

3. Wherefore, brethren, look ye out among you seven men of honest report, *full* of the Holy Ghost and wisdom, whom we may appoint over this business. (Acts 6:3)

4. And the saying pleased the whole multitude: and they chose Stephen, a man *full* of faith and of the Holy Ghost ... And Stepehen full of faith and power, did great wonders and miracles among the people. (Acts 6:5,8)

5. And the disciples were *filled* with joy, and with the Holy Ghost. (Acts 13:52)

6. Now the God of hope *fill* you with all joy and peace in believing, that ye may abound in hope, through the power of the Holy Ghost. (Rom. 15:13)

7. And be not drunk with wine, wherein is excess; but be *filled* with the Spirit; Speaking to yourselves in psalms and hymns and spiritual songs, singing and making melody in your heart to the Lord; Giving thanks always for all things unto God and the Father in the name of our Lord Jesus Christ. (Eph. 5:18-20)